Calvin Johnson: The Inspiring Story of One of Football's Greatest Wide Receivers

An Unauthorized Biography

By: Clayton Geoffreys

Copyright © 2016 by Calvintir Books, LLC

All rights reserved. Neither this book nor any portion thereof may be reproduced or used in any manner whatsoever without the express written permission. Published in the United States of America.

Disclaimer: The following book is for entertainment and informational purposes only. The information presented is without contract or any type of guarantee assurance. While every caution has been taken to provide accurate and current information, it is solely the reader's responsibility to check all information contained in this article before relying upon it. Neither the author nor publisher can be held accountable for any errors or omissions.

Under no circumstances will any legal responsibility or blame be held against the author or publisher for any reparation, damages, or monetary loss due to the information presented, either directly or indirectly. This book is not intended as legal or medical advice. If any such specialized advice is needed, seek a qualified individual for help.

Trademarks are used without permission. Use of the trademark is not authorized by, associated with, or sponsored by the trademark owners. All trademarks and brands used within this book are used with no intent to infringe on the trademark owners and only used for clarifying purposes.

This book is not sponsored by or affiliated with the National Football Association, its teams, the players, or anyone involved with them.

Visit my website at www.claytongeoffreys.com
Cover photo by Mike Morbeck is licensed under CC BY 2.0 / modified from original

Table of Contents

Foreword 1

Introduction 3

Chapter 1: Childhood and Early Life 7

Chapter 2: High School Football 11

Chapter 3: College Football 17

    2004 Season 17

    2005 Season 23

    2006 Season 28

Chapter 4: NFL Career 38

    2007 NFL Draft 38

    2007 Season 42

    2008 Season 48

    2009 Season 53

    2010 Season 60

2011 Season..66

2012 Season..73

2013 Season..78

2014 Season..85

2015 Season..91

Chapter 5: Johnson's Retirement from the NFL 98

Chapter 6: How Johnson Compares to All-Time Greatest Receivers..109

Chapter 7: Johnson's Charitable Work 112

Chapter 8: Personal Life..117

Chapter 9: Johnson's Overall Legacy 121

Final Word/About the Author 124

References 127

Foreword

One of the greatest wide receivers to ever play the game, Calvin Johnson Jr. had an illustrious career playing professional football. A second overall pick in the 2007 NFL Draft, Johnson retired in 2016 as a six-time Pro Bowl selection, three-time First-team All-Pro, and the holder of several league records. Calvin Johnson's story is one of perseverance and hard work. Since entering the league a high prospect, Johnson demonstrated great poise and professionalism throughout his career that led him to become one of the most successful wide receivers in recent years. Thank you for purchasing *Calvin Johnson: The Inspiring Story of One of Football's Greatest Wide Receivers*. In this unauthorized biography, we will learn Calvin Johnson's incredible life story and impact on the game of football. Hope you enjoy and if you do, please do not forget to leave a review!

Also, check out my website at claytongeoffreys.com to join my exclusive list where I let you know about my latest books. To thank you for your purchase, you can go to my site to download a free copy of *33 Life Lessons: Success*

Principles, Career Advice & Habits of Successful People. In the book, you'll learn from some of the greatest thought leaders of different industries on what it takes to become successful and how to live a great life.

Cheers,

Clayton Geoffreys

Visit me at www.claytongeoffreys.com

Introduction

There are only so many athletes in professional sports who some experts might call "freaks of nature." The Detroit Lions have had two of them in their franchise history. The first was Barry Sanders, who ran from 1989 to 1998 and collected more than 15,000 rushing yards. He had retired near the prime of his career, not long after having a season with 2,053 yards and 11 touchdowns in the 1997 season.[i] Back then, some people wondered why he would leave professional football while still showing signs of being one of the best running backs that were playing at the time. Many people felt it was because the franchise only went to the playoffs five times with just one win that sent the Lions to the NFC Championship.

Detroit would have another chance of having another freak of nature athlete that would prove be arguably the best wide receiver the NFL has ever seen. It all started in 2007 when Calvin Johnson, Jr. would enter the league with a lot of attention coming out of Georgia Institute of Technology – better known as Georgia Tech – as a junior, and many thought he was the top prospect in the 2007 NFL Draft. It took some time, but Johnson would become a target for the Lions who many would describe as a total package that started with having the size that made him tower over the defending cornerbacks and safeties around the league – he was six-foot-five, weighed just under 240 pounds, and had colossal hands. But unlike most men his height and size, Johnson was faster than with a 40-yard dash time of under 4.4 seconds. It was no surprise that he was a genuinely special kind of athlete, which many of his coaches would say publically, including Jim Schwartz – a former head coach who had a chance to work with Johnson during his first playoff run in 2011. But it was also noticed by other coaches, like Chan Gailey, who commented that Johnson was a bigger and faster player than anyone else he had ever played with – whether it was in high school, college, or even in the NFL. "It was a total mismatch," Gailey said.

He would put up a lot of high numbers which seemed more like something that would be accumulated on a create-a-player on a football video game. That might be part of the reason why Johnson would find himself on the cover of a video game during his highly successful career in the NFL.

At the same time, he was a positive role model who brought his Christian faith into what he did off the field – creating a foundation that helped children in need from the areas he was connected with – Atlanta, Georgia and Detroit, Michigan. While many modern wide receivers in the NFL would come into the league extremely confident and might have a negative aura around them – i.e. Terrell Owens, Chad Johnson and Randy Moss – Calvin Johnson had no negativity around him. Even though his nickname, "Megatron," was that of the main villain in the Transformers franchise, Johnson was the type of professional athlete that was the perfect role model. He put in the hard work to excel in his sport, took wins with humility and losses with grace, and was dedicated to everything he did both on and off the field.

His career ended abruptly after the 2015 season, but there were a number of reasons that make this wide receiver arguably one of the greatest to ever go up for a catch in the end zone. There are not too many players in the Pro Football Hall of Fame who could say they had the physical abilities to be able to leap over three defenders and come down with a catch for a crucial touchdown.

Chapter 1: Childhood and Early Life

Calvin Johnson, Jr., was born on September 25, 1985, to his parents Calvin, Sr. and Arica while the family was living in Newnan, Georgia. The city rests in the Northwest part of the state inside Coweta County and had a population of only approximately 40,000 residents. It was within an hour's drive of Atlanta, Georgia. The family would move to Tyrone, Georgia, which was not too far from Calvin's birth town. Johnson would be the second of four children in the household. They were raised by a father who worked for a local railroad company, and a mom who acted as an administrator for a school system in Atlanta.[ii]

Another thing about the young Johnson was that he was a standout youth athlete who showed at an early age that he was able to have a good amount of speed with great coordination and body control that came naturally to him. But even at this young age, Johnson was always one of the big advocates of being a good sport, whether he won or lost. This was no surprise because his parents were of Christian faith, and their values rubbed off on all of their children, which explains a lot about the kind nature he always maintained throughout college and even in the NFL.

Both of the parents placed their primary focus on their Christian faith while also telling their children how important having an education was. One of Johnson's sisters completed medical school to become a doctor. In the end, his father would tell the New York Times during a feature on Johnson that the family had a zero-tolerance policy when it came to foolishness.[iii]

Because of where he lived and having a childhood where he was involved in sports, Johnson was a big Atlanta sports fan – especially the Atlanta Braves. What might surprise some football fans is the fact that Johnson was more into America's pastime as a child and often played baseball as his main sport of choice, starting at the age of five.[iv] During his childhood, Johnson was able to see the Braves have some of their best years in team history with 14 consecutive National League East Division championships after being the worst team in baseball in 1990. Johnson's main favorite at the time was first baseman Fred McGriff because he had longer arms and often held a baseball camp that the soon-to-be NFL star would remember attending.

Johnson had some great baseball memories as a child that included watching Sid Bream slide home for the winning run to help the Braves defeat the Pittsburgh Pirates for the N.L. pennant in 1992. At the same time, he also watched baseball and noted the respect he had for Ken Griffey, Jr., who was a star during that period with the Seattle Mariners.

Despite his love for baseball, Johnson was excelling in football the most out of all of the sports he played as a child. However, his mother virtually forbid her son Calvin from going into full pads during his grade school years, which meant that Johnson did not get a chance to play full-contact football until he entered the seventh grade.

By then, he was the tallest student in his class after a massive growth spurt caused him reach six feet tall. This was a trait that got many of the coaches on his team in middle school excited, and they were sending the word up to the folks that would soon receive him at the high school level. Someone hitting six feet before fully maturing in high school was a good sign that they were going to have a chance to be a great wide receiver.

Chapter 2: High School Football

In 2000, Johnson started his high school years at Sandy Creek High School in Tyrone, Georgia, a more rural suburban city near Atlanta. He was already standing at six feet while still in middle school. He would hit close to his peak height of about six-foot-four by the time he was a sophomore at Sandy Creek.[v] He was used to being the tall man on the practice team for a high school program that had done well for many years. Chip Walker, who was an assistant head coach for the football team during Johnson's time at Sandy Creek, noted that he was a very tall kid who did not have a lot of weight. That changed by the time he graduated as a six-foot-four, 200-pound wide receiver who attracted some national scouting attention.[vi]

While he got some playing time as a sophomore, he was mostly kept on the sidelines and still developing as a young receiver who had some respectable height at the time. However during his junior year, his coaches started to notice the changes between his sophomore and junior season when his body began to grow and mature overall.[vii] During the 2002 season as a junior at Sandy Creek,

Johnson had 646 yards and ten touchdowns accumulated on just 34 catches on the year.[viii] During that season, one of his former coaches Walker, who is now the current head coach at Sandy Creek, recalled a highlight during a game against Woodward Academy, which was Sandy Creek's biggest rival at the time. After coming back from a huge deficit, Johnson was able to make a big catch on a throw into the end zone that was not thrown very well in the first place. Walker explained that, in what would become typical Megatron fashion on Sundays, Johnson was able to wrap himself around the defending cornerback and undercut him to get a catch for the game-tying touchdown – a game that would later be won by Sandy Creek in overtime.

It was during his senior season in 2003 that Johnson started to make a huge impact in football. While he only had 40 catches that year, he finished with 736 yards and eight touchdowns.[ix] It was a year to remember for the team as they were able to clinch their first regional title in 2003, which would be the first of several the school has won since then. Some people might feel that Johnson might have motivated the community to see what a winning culture is like. Johnson received a few honors as one of the top-rated high school players in the state of Georgia, including being named as a first-team selection for the All-State Class AAAA team by the Atlanta Journal-Constitution. It was not the only time the newspaper spoke highly of Johnson, considering that before the start of the 2003 season, Johnson was part of their Super 11 preseason roster for that year.

There was a lot more attention coming to the Sandy Creek community in Georgia as there were a lot more college scouts coming out to more Patriot games. Johnson was considered the top prospect coming out of the state for college football while still finding himself the 12th overall in the Southeast region and 37th nationally by high school recruiting website Rivals.com. Several schools were looking into Johnson, but the top four college football programs that offered the five-star wide receiving recruit included the Notre Dame Fighting Irish, the Miami Hurricanes, the Georgia Bulldogs, and the Georgia Tech Yellow Jackets. Most were projecting that the two in-state schools had the inside track on Johnson since they had the home field advantage in recruiting. But there was a lot of attention for the Sandy Creek star because nearly every high school football writer was placing Johnson in the top 10 of the nation's wide receivers and at a good position in the country's top 100. On January 12, 2004, Johnson made the decision to commit to playing for the Yellow Jackets.

The interesting thing to note about Johnson's recruitment to Georgia Tech is that the school wanted to bring him in not only for football, but for baseball as well. In April 2004, Johnson was placed through some drills that included a 60-yard dash that he completed in about 6.54 seconds. This made sense for someone who ran a 40-yard dash in 4.27 seconds for football drills.[x] It was not considered a big deal until someone mentioned that sort of time matched up with another great two-sport athlete – Deion Sanders. Later on, college baseball scouts brought some wooden bats to see what Johnson could do regarding hitting. High school and college baseball usually feature aluminum bats. Some people feel that if you can hit far with wooden bats, you could continue developing your overall hitting abilities in college and eventually professional leagues. On that April afternoon recalled by the Atlanta Journal-Constitution, Johnson was able to send a few baseballs well into the girls' softball field that was beyond the baseball field's left field fence.

Georgia Tech was excited to have someone playing two sports since the school wanted to continue being competitive in both and there were baseball scouts interested in Johnson as a potential shortstop. It was a game that Johnson had started playing at the very young age of 5, following the hometown Atlanta Braves make their worst-to-first jump in 1991 that began a 14-year streak of winning the National League's East Division in Major League Baseball[xi].

However, his mother Arica Johnson stepped in and played the mom role, making it clear that Johnson was not going to focus on baseball. This included telling people he was not going to enter Major League Baseball's annual draft where high school kids could be selected to enter their minor league development systems.[xii] The problem she saw was that playing two sports while going to college might put too much on her son's plate, and that can be pretty overwhelming for someone who wants to earn a good education. That was the point where Johnson's prolific baseball career ended after he graduated from Sandy Creek High School in the spring of 2004.

Chapter 3: College Football[xiii]

2004 Season

Calvin Johnson was a freshman who was able to go straight into the field. He did not have to be placed on a redshirt status in his first year on the Georgia Tech campus in 2004. He had only a few moments to make some plays in his first game with the team on September 4, 2004, during a 28-7 win over Samford at home. Johnson had just two catches for 45 yards.

However, Johnson was able to make an immediate impact against Atlantic Coast Conference rivals in the Clemson Tigers on September 11, 2004, on the road in South Carolina. It was a memorable game where the Yellow Jackets were trailing by 10 points in the competition's final two minutes and was completed by an exciting series of events. This included a bad snap on Clemson's punt with 30 seconds left that should have led the Tigers to clinch the home win. However, the snap skipped on the turf past the punter Cole Cason, who had to fall on the ball on Clemson's 11-yard-line. This set up a chance for Georgia

Tech quarterback Reggie Ball to complete the 11-yard touchdown to Johnson for the 28-24 win. Johnson was able to get the touchdown catch on what resembled a jump ball in basketball with members of Clemson's secondary defense.[xiv]

The win over the Tigers allowed Johnson to showcase his overall talents on the field after he caught eight passes for 127 yards that game. In addition to the game-winning touchdown, Johnson also caught a 37-yard pass from Ball for a first quarter touchdown and also had a touchdown nearly two minutes before the game-winning goal. It was a big game for the young receiver, but being young also means that there is room for some improvement. The young Yellow Jackets star had a couple of slow games in the next two weeks during some heartbreaking losses for Georgia Tech. During a 34-13 loss on the road to the North Carolina Tar Heels on September 18, 2004, Johnson had two catches for 45 yards again. But he had only 10 yards on two catches on October 2, 2004, at home against then fourth-ranked Miami Hurricanes in a 27-3 loss, a game where the Yellow Jackets only gained about 230 yards on offense.

While the Georgia Tech offense struggled, Johnson would start to find his groove in October with three catches for 76 yards during a big 20-7 win on the road at Maryland on October 9, 2004. It was a game where Georgia Tech's defense truly stood out with holding the Terrapins to under 100 total offensive yards while Ball completed 11 passes for 197 yards and an 11-yard touchdown pass to Nate Curry. Johnson made big catches that included key plays that helped continue drives to keep the Yellow Jacket offense on the field.

On October 16, 2004, Johnson had some key plays after having six receptions for 92 yards during a 24-7 win over the Duke Blue Devils. Johnson had a 20-yard touchdown catch from Ball's arm in the first minute of the second quarter and would get another touchdown on a 13-yard pass in the third quarter. He would score another touchdown on a nine-yard pass in the first quarter of a 34-20 loss to the Virginia Tech Hokies on October 28, 2004, a game where he finished with four receptions for 51 yards.

Johnson would make big plays in other games where he might not have scored in the end zone.

Two of his earliest highlight plays were during the go-ahead touchdown drive in the fourth quarter that allowed the Yellow Jackets to earn the 24-14 win over the North Carolina State Wolfpack on November 6, 2004. In the touchdown drive that ended with a one-yard pass from Ball to Levon Thomas, Johnson had a one-handed grab on a third down with four yards to go to extend the drive that earned the top play of the day on ESPN's SportsCenter that night[xv]. Moments later, he would make a big catch for 27 yards that brought the Yellow Jackets to N.C. State's four-yard-line. He would also draw a pass interference penalty that brought them closer to the goal line to set up the touchdown throw.

As the season continued, Johnson would accumulate some big numbers in several different games to help Georgia Tech earn bowl eligibility for the 2004 season. Johnson had a season-high 131 receiving yards on six catches on November 13, 2004, during a 30-10 win over the Connecticut Huskies. But the Yellow Jackets would end the regular season with back-to-back losses to the 18th ranked Virginia Cavaliers (30-10) on November 20, 2004, in a game where Johnson had five receptions for 108 yards. The next game was a heartbreaking loss to the eighth-ranked Georgia Bulldogs, 19-13, on November 27, 2004. It was a defensive battle where Georgia Tech could only muster about 194 yards in their offense; Johnson could only get 44 yards on his five receptions.

Despite the struggles near the end of the season, Georgia Tech still had bowl eligibility with the minimal requirement of six wins, which earned an invitation to the Champs Sports Bowl held December 21, 2004, in Orlando, Florida. It was a chance for sophomore quarterback Ball to stand out with 12 of 19 completions for 207 yards and a running back performance where P.J. Daniels had 17 carries for 119 yards and two touchdowns to give Georgia Tech the 51-14 win over the Syracuse Orange. This game was the worst loss Syracuse had suffered since the 1953 Orange Bowl to the Alabama Crimson Tide (61-6)[xvi].

Johnson had some big plays of his own that started with catching a 10-yard pass from Ball in the first quarter to make the game 14-6 for the Yellow Jackets lead. But just before halftime, Johnson had two big plays to result in a touchdown that made the score 35-6 at the break. It started with Johnson getting past Syracuse's Tanard Jackson for a fantastic reception over safety Diamond Ferri that would give him a majority of his 61 receiving yards on the game. Johnson would have the final play of the touchdown drive on the end around rush for a five-yard sprint to the end zone.

It was a great game to put a highlight on Johnson's freshman season with Georgia Tech where he led the team with 48 catches, 837 yards, and seven touchdowns. All three were freshman records in the school's history. Throughout the season, Johnson was named the ACC's Rookie of the Week for his individual efforts against the Tigers, Blue Devils, UConn Huskies and the Cavaliers, an achievement that no one else in conference history was able to do more than three times in a single season. Johnson was also named to the first team All-ACC and the first team of the Freshman All-American list for 2004. There was excitement around the Georgia Tech campus with high hopes of how Johnson was going to continue to grow as the Yellow Jackets' top receiving threat moving forward. But little did anyone know how dominant Johnson would be playing in the Yellow Jackets' uniform for the next few seasons.

2005 Season

It did not take long for Johnson to build upon his breakout freshman season as he was easily a central focus point by opposing defenses. They knew what he was capable of after he helped the Yellow Jackets earn a decisive bowl victory over Syracuse the year before. But Johnson would continue to show that he was something special – a freak of athletic nature if you will.

In the season opener against then 15th-ranked Auburn on September 3, 2005, he had 66 yards on four catches that included a 35-yard touchdown pass from Ball on Georgia Tech's opening drive to help earn the upset victory on the road, 23-14. Johnson also forced the Tigers' defense to interfere with catches that would have otherwise been breakaway touchdowns. It was just the first sign of Johnson being a force to be reckoned with during the 2005 season. Georgia Tech was showing how good they could be overall on offense and with a very stingy defense that had four interceptions against Auburn quarterback Brandon Cox.[xvii]

After collecting six catches for 114 yards during a 27-21 win over North Carolina, Johnson had to play with the backup quarterback Taylor Bennett after Bell was out with an injury. It did not stop Johnson from being open enough for a 42-yard touchdown pass from Bennett for a touchdown in the 28-13 win over the visiting UConn Huskies on September 17, 2005; one of Johnson's three catches for 75 yards on the day.

As the ACC schedule started to ramp up for Georgia Tech, the Yellow Jackets were suffering some severe losses which began with a 51-7 rout at the hands of Virginia Tech on September 24, 2005. Ball returned to action, but struggled with 11 out of 27 passing for 143 yards and two interceptions. Johnson was the lone positive note in the loss as he set career-high marks for yards in a game with 123 yards on just five receptions, including the lone touchdown on an 11-yard pass from Ball. It was the only touchdown that the Virginia Tech defense had given up in about 14 quarters since the opening drive of their season-opener. But it was the only drive where Georgia Tech was able to get anything going. As running back P.J. Daniels said after the game, the loss to the Hokies felt like "an old-fashioned beat-down."[xviii]

Georgia Tech would look a lot stronger in their next game with 443 yards of total offense at home on October 6, 2005. However, they would fall to the North Carolina State Wolfpack, 17-14. Johnson would set new career highs with ten catches for 130 yards that were highlighted by a 27-yard touchdown catch from Ball in the third quarter to break their scoreless drought from the first half.

But Johnson would help keep the Yellow Jackets in being eligible for a bowl berth after three straight wins at Duke (35-10), vs. Clemson (10-9), and against Wake Forest (30-17). During those three wins that clinched bowl eligibility, Johnson had 12 receptions for a total of 217 receiving yards. He had one touchdown that came off a three-yard pass from Ball in the early part of the second half of the win over Wake Forest. After breaking back into the national rankings at number 24, the Yellow Jackets would suffer their third loss of the season on November 12, 2005, to the Virginia Cavaliers, 27-17, on the road. Johnson was held to just 41 yards on four catches. But he would collect another 89 yards on six receptions to lead Georgia Tech's receivers to help them get a huge upset of the Miami Hurricanes, who were ranked third in the country at the time, 14-10, on November 19, 2005.

Johnson would score another touchdown during the final game of the regular season, the Yellow Jackets' annual in-state matchup with rival Georgia; it was on a quick two-yard pass into the end zone by Ball that he came down with to give Georgia Tech the early 7-0. But the teams battled back and forth before Bulldogs quarterback D.J. Shockley completed a 19-yard pass to Bryan McClendon for the go-ahead touchdown for the 14-7 final score. It was a tough game for Georgia Tech's passing offense as Ball completed only 18 of 35 throws for 155 yards and had two interceptions against him.

The Yellow Jackets would receive an invitation to play in the Emerald Bowl on December 29, 2005, in San Francisco,

California against the Utah Utes out of the Mountain West Conference. Utah defensive back Eric Weddle shined throughout all facets of the game that included gaining 23 rushing yards and even helped with a fake field goal attempt. But the biggest impact was defending Johnson and holding him to just two catches for 19 yards – as well as deflecting another pass in Johnson's direction – as Utah would get the decisive 38-10 win over Georgia Tech.[xix]

Despite the Yellow Jackets finishing 7-5 again, Johnson was making a big name for himself throughout the world of college football. He finished the season with 54 receptions for 888 yards and six touchdowns, leading the team in all three categories. He was also second in the conference with an average of 74 receiving yards per game and fifth in the conference with four-and-a-half receptions per game.

While his numbers took a big jump, Johnson also became just the first Georgia Tech player to be named to the first-team All-American list since offensive tackle Chris Brown was selected in 2000. Johnson was the first Yellow Jackets receiver to be on the All-American list since Billy Martin was honored in 1963. He received several conference honors for the second consecutive season while also being named a semifinalist for the Biletnikoff Award, which was given out to the nation's top college football wide receiver. Football fans outside of the ACC were starting to take notice as he continued to show up regularly on the weekly highlight tapes on sports television shows, even having plays in the top-10 highlights from the 2005 season. However, his junior season would turn out to be his best.

2006 Season

The attention that Johnson was getting at Georgia Tech entering his junior year with the Yellow Jackets was fascinating because the belief was that he rarely dropped passes. Johnson could only recall "maybe" three passes he feels should have been caught, but fell to the turf.[xx] But it wasn't just his natural ability to get the ball, regardless of how many defenders were on him. He had the size of a giant at six-foot-five and was just under 240 pounds in weight. Some of his coaches commented that someone that size should not be able to twist his body counterclockwise to grab a ball thrown behind him. Nor would they expect an agile receiver at a much smaller size to have a chance at that kind of play. But Johnson was not like most receivers, and he would prove it again in the 2006 season.

The season started off at home with a marquee matchup opportunity against the Notre Dame Fighting Irish at home, a team that was ranked second in the nation. Johnson would have Georgia Tech's lone touchdown after catching a jump ball pass from Ball for a four-yard connection just before the end of the first quarter. A field goal from Travis Bell put the Yellow Jackets up 10-0 before a few key touchdown drives by Brady Quinn gave the Irish the narrow 14-10 decision on September 2, 2006. Johnson accounted for nearly all of the passing yards with 111 on seven receptions; the second most receiving yards for Georgia Tech was 10 yards by James Johnson – no relation.

The Yellow Jackets would bounce back the very next week against the lesser Division I team, Samford, at home on September 9, 2006. Johnson only had to take the field for about half of the game as he had two key touchdown catches in the second quarter of five and 11 yards to help Georgia Tech put their opponents away early in a 38-6 win.

He also had a chance to show his abilities on the end-around rushing attack with a 21-yard run as his main highlight during a 35-20 win over Troy on September 16, 2006. Johnson had just two catches for nine yards in the game. With the small numbers in the some of the early games, there was a little bit of doubt whether he let some of the national attention distract him from continuing his progression. He was about to prove them wrong, and the Virginia Cavaliers were going to be on the receiving end of that statement.

Johnson had a career-high with 165 yards on just six receptions to help the Yellow Jackets get the 24-7 win at home against Virginia for a key conference victory on September 21, 2006. There were some doubts as to whether Johnson was 100 percent because he had some pains in his left leg that were not making the pre-game warmups any easier.[xxi] It did not help that he barely practiced during a very short week, but he admits that once the game got going, there was no pain. Johnson would do well enough to finish with six catches for 165 yards that featured two big plays where single-coverage from

Virginia's defense was blown. The first was on a 58-yard touchdown pass from Ball with just a minute left in the first half, which came after pulling away from Virginia's Jamaal Jackson on a quick slant to the outside before making the catch in the middle of the field. In an early third quarter drive, Johnson was able to get past the one defender for a 66-yard touchdown reception to give Georgia Tech the 24-0 win. This came after a good stutter step along the sideline caught Virginia's Marcus Hamilton off guard and then cut to the inside got Johnson away from safety Tony Franklin. After the game, Johnson told reporters that, when he lines up before the play and sees just one man defending him, he loves the opportunity. So one would think that opposing defenses would start having two defenders to keep him in check, right?

Over the past few years, the Yellow Jackets had lost in big blowouts to the Virginia Tech Hokies. So when they went to their stadium in Blacksburg, Virginia, on September 30, 2006, Georgia Tech had a little bit of extra motivation to earn an upset against the team that was ranked 11th in the country at the time. While Virginia Tech had more offensive yards in the game (381-325), the Yellow Jackets created two big fumbles that were recovered for touchdowns to give Georgia Tech the 38-27 upset win. One of the biggest plays came on the second offensive drive for Georgia Tech when Ball was able to connect with Johnson on a short pass that turned into a big 53-yard touchdown as Johnson was able to run past three Virginia Tech defenders without being touched at all.[xxii] Johnson had one other goal in the game and finished with 115 yards on six receptions.

Johnson's success would continue as he had another ten receptions for 133 yards and one touchdown during a 27-23 win over the Maryland Terrapins on October 7, 2006. This was followed up with another 68 yards and one touchdown in a 30-23 win against the Miami Hurricanes on October 28, 2006; a game where Johnson even completed a seven-yard pass in the game on a trick play.

The combination of Ball moving to Johnson would strike again during a road win over the North Carolina State Wolfpack on November 4, 2006, where the Yellow Jackets combined for 409 offensive yards in the 31-23 win. After

Ball had scrambled 28 yards on the opening drive for Georgia Tech to get a first down, he was able to find Johnson behind the Wolfpack's secondary for the 25-yard touchdown score.[xxiii] Ball would later connect with Johnson for a 43-yard touchdown before the end of the first quarter. This forced N.C. State to put a second defender on Johnson for double-coverage, although he finished with a career high of 168 yards on nine receptions. This allowed Georgia Tech's rushing attack to total nearly 200 yards, led by Tashard Choice's 164 yards on the ground.

After a game where he had another 78 yards and two touchdowns in a win over the Duke Blue Devils, the Yellow Jackets would fall into a bit of a losing streak. It started on November 25, 2006, in a 15-12 loss to the Bulldogs. Georgia Tech was held to less than 190 yards of offense. Johnson had just two catches for 13 yards while Ball was held to only six completions out of 22 throws for 42 yards and two interceptions. Despite the loss, it was their only regular season loss in the ACC, which gave them a berth in the conference championship on December 2, 2006, in Jacksonville, Florida. But the Demon Deacons would make life hard on Georgia Tech's Ball, who finished with only nine out of 29 completions for 129 yards and two interceptions as the Yellow Jackets lost 9-6. Johnson had eight of those completions for 117 yards, but could not find the end zone.

Wake Forest's defense was able to make big plays that included Riley Swanson's interception in the fourth quarter that helped set up one of the two field goals that gave the Demon Deacons the trip to the Orange Bowl that season. Johnson had two drops that would have been big plays if he brought the ball in, which he had made a career of doing at Georgia Tech. One of those drops ended up in the hands of Wake Forest's Swanson for that momentum-shifting interception. The loss meant that Georgia Tech would have to settle for the Gator Bowl and return to Jacksonville, Florida, even though Gator Bowl officials were hoping otherwise.[xxiv]

The rumors began to swirl about whether Johnson would declare for the upcoming NFL Draft after finishing his junior season, which meant forgoing his senior year at Georgia Tech[xxv]. That might have been a big motivator for him having one of his best collegiate games on January 1, 2007, against the West Virginia Mountaineers in a 38-35 loss in the 2007 Gator Bowl. Despite often being double and triple-covered throughout the game and despite having backup Taylor Bennett make only his second career start due to an injury to Ball, Johnson made several big catches to keep Georgia Tech in the game. This included a conversion on third down and 32 yards to go in the third quarter where Johnson had to jump for the ball between two Mountaineers. Johnson also had a 31-yard touchdown catch in the first quarter and a 48-yard touchdown catch in the early minutes of the second quarter. Overall, he had nine receptions for a new college career high of 186 yards.

But West Virginia was powered by a rushing offense that had 311 yards on the ground with quarterback Pat White gaining 145 yards and a touchdown and Owen Schmitt having 109 yards and two touchdowns of his own. It was a bitter loss for the 9-4 Yellow Jackets, and it did not sit well with Johnson, who later admitted that the decision to leave for the NFL was a little tougher after losing in the Gator Bowl.

Johnson finished his junior season with 1,202 receiving yards on 76 receptions and a total of 15 touchdowns, all of which were collegiate career highs for the season. It was enough for Johnson to receive the Biletnikoff Award for being the country's best wide receiver. He was also named the ACC Player of the Year and was also considered a unanimous first team All-American athlete by several publications like the Associated Press and the Football Writers Association of America. However, there were many factors to consider before deciding whether to stay one more season with Georgia Tech or make the transition to professional football. Johnson was already the leading receiver in school history with a total of about 2,927 yards in his three seasons with Georgia Tech.

The question would ultimately be what Johnson would do moving forward after the loss in the 2007 Gator Bowl. Granted, Johnson spoke publically about his desire to finish his business management degree from Georgia Tech, so there was at least some deep consideration by Johnson. However, it was not long after the Gator Bowl that he would come to that decision. On January 8, 2007, Johnson would officially announce that he would be skipping his senior year at Georgia Tech to declare for the National Football League's 2007 Draft that would take place months later.[xxvi] The news was announced during a press conference with his family. And who could blame Johnson, especially considering that he was being placed at the top spot on a midseason draft projection by Sports Illustrated in February 2007?[xxvii] There several scouts who were looking at the young receiver out of Tyrone, Georgia, particularly after he put up plenty of impressive numbers in 2006 against some of the country's best defensive units.

Chapter 4: NFL Career[xxviii]

2007 NFL Draft

There was no question by any of the experts whether Johnson was one of the best athletes to enter the NFL Draft, but it there was a reason he was placed as the top pick on a lot of the boards predicted by different NFL Draft experts. Johnson would have an additional workout for NFL team scouts at Georgia Tech later that month, which included a 40-yard dash time of 4.33 seconds and a vertical jump of 43 inches. He also had an 11-foot standing broad jump that caught more attention from different teams that were in need of a deep threat wide receiver who was not afraid to go up and outmuscle defenders to grab a pass at clutch moments.[xxix] One of Georgia Tech's speed and conditioning coaches, Tom Shaw, commented that he believes Johnson is the type of athlete that would not be a bad pick for anyone because of his lack of negative marks against him and many positive physical attributes.

During the NFL's Rookie Combine in February 2007, it was reported that Johnson was considered an athlete that surpassed the abilities of Randy Moss, who was seen as an athletic freak of nature in his right.[xxx] There were some concerns at first when he came into the combine in Indianapolis, Indiana, where he was reported at 239 pounds; more than 10 pounds heavier than many expected, and that was what led to people to worrying about a case similar to Mike Williams' struggles in Detroit. The former USC Trojan star receiver tried to enter early into the league and then debuted with the Lions much heavier and slower than expected.

But the six-foot-five, 239-pound Johnson had one of the fastest times at the combine with just 4.35 seconds. The concept of someone that size who was moving that quickly sounded like a very scary situation for cornerbacks and safeties in the NFL, who were potentially going to have to try to defend someone like Johnson. He felt confident that he was one of the better athletes in the field of NFL prospects, but he was also attracting scouts because he did not have a lot of unnecessary baggage. Johnson's record was clean and without any crimes, violent past, or addictions to substances of any kind. Johnson was showing a work ethic that was described as being similar to other great wide receivers in the NFL like Marvin Harrison and Terrell Owens. But if that was not impressive enough, Johnson also had a vertical jump of about 45 inches. There was still some competition with some decent receivers that included Jason Hill from Washington State having a 40-yard dash of 4.32 seconds and Robert Meachem catching almost every pass that was thrown his way during drills. Gil Brandt of NFL.com wrote that Johnson had one of the best broad jumps he had ever seen during a rookie combine when he improved his personal best to 11 feet seven inches.[xxxi]

However, Johnson was seemingly the perfect combination of speed, agility, and size that was rarely seen. Someone who was built like Johnson and with the abilities he displayed in college and during the workouts was hard for anyone to imagine. The last wide receiver to have the type of impact he was having was Randy Moss back in 1998, although Moss was not considered a top-10 draft pick because of a few reasons. Firstly, he was coming out of the tiny Mid-American Conference program in Marshall. Secondly, Moss was in the same draft as highly-rated prospects like Peyton Manning, Ryan Leaf, and Charles Woodson[xxxii].

But that was in 1998, and the 2007 NFL Draft was held during a time where the internet made tracking statistics much easier for football fans. Scouts were more likely to hear about someone who was not competing for a national championship or one of the major bowl games held on New Year's Day. Johnson was also at Georgia Tech and played top level competition against other ACC programs like Virginia Tech, Clemson, and North Carolina. He had a lot more attention than someone like Moss had when he was trying to be noticed during the combines and workouts.

What was interesting is that the number one draft pick in 2007 belonged to the Oakland Raiders, who many were expecting would select the wide receiver. But the Raiders went with Louisiana State University quarterback JaMarcus Russell instead, who had some questions as a larger framed quarterback who was weighing in at about 260 pounds. Johnson would be chosen second overall in the draft by the Detroit Lions, which made him the ninth Georgia Tech player to be selected in the first round and the highest selected in school history.[xxxiii] Rumors were going around that the Lions were going to trade Johnson to the Tampa Bay Buccaneers, but the rumors were quickly debunked by Lions general manager Matt Millen when he stated that Detroit was going to keep Johnson with the Lions.[xxxiv]

Johnson was believed to provide some much-needed star power and help for the Lions moving forward after several years of losing, including a 3-13 season in 2006. Detroit was hoping to see a much stronger team, which led the Lions draft quarterback Drew Stanton out of Michigan State and defensive end Ikaika Alama-Francis out of Hawaii, both in the second round. But Johnson was already being welcomed by the Detroit sports fans as he was invited to throw out the first pitch at a Detroit Tigers game a few days after the NFL Draft at Comerica Park.[xxxv]

2007 Season

Johnson's start with the Lions was a little bit rocky, but not of his fault. The league had Johnson attend the NFL Rookie Premiere held in Los Angeles, California, in May 2007. The event was considered to be a primary marketing tool for the league which promotes some of their top incoming players to the NFL for the season in the upcoming fall. Johnson was one of the several players who were going to miss the early rookie minicamp that was starting around that time.[xxxvi] This led to the Lions rescheduling their minicamp to accommodate the situation for their incoming first-round draft pick. The team was showing that they were committed to Johnson being one of their franchise's top stars, and it was demonstrated financially on August 3, 2007, when the team was able to have Johnson sign a contract for six years. Granted it required Johnson to hold off on camp in order to get a maximum contract, which led to him missing about eight days of the preseason training camp. His agent James "Bus" Cook was able to help him earn a $64 million deal that included about $27 million in guaranteed money upon signing, which made Johnson the third-highest paid player in Detroit Lions history, as well as the highest paid receiver in the NFL at the time.[xxxvii] The contract also included another $4.5 million in bonuses that he could also earn.

The first practice Johnson attended was gaining a lot of attention, which led to the Lions making his first practice the first one open to the general public since 2002; their first days at the current headquarters in Allen Park, Michigan. Fans were excited to see what the newest franchise star was going to be capable of, especially knowing that he was talented enough from his days at Georgia Tech. His time was limited in preseason games as per usual, but he did have some deep passes that included a 24-yard reception in his NFL preseason debut on August 9, 2007, against the Cincinnati Bengals.

Johnson did not start in his first game of the NFL on September 9, 2007, while the Lions visited the Oakland Raiders, but he did make an immediate impact with four receptions for 70 yards and caught a 16-yard pass from Lions quarterback Jon Kitna in the third quarter for his first career touchdown.[xxxviii] The Lions would hold off the Raiders by a score of 36-21. Johnson would have another four receptions for 61 yards during the Lions big 20-17 win over the Minnesota Vikings at home on September 16, 2007. Johnson had his second career touchdown after catching a seven-yard throw from backup quarterback J.T. O'Sullivan.

Johnson had to leave the game after just two catches for 58 yards due to a bruised lower back in the Lions' 56-21 loss to the Philadelphia Eagles, who were looking like one of the greatest offensive units of all time with players like Donovan McNabb at quarterback throwing for 381 yards. Kitna did have 446 yards and a 91-yard touchdown pass to Roy Williams, but the problems with Detroit seemed to be on the defensive side of the ball. Johnson's injury would have a small impact as he missed the Lions' home game against the Chicago Bears on September 30, 2007, which Detroit won 37-27. Johnson would return to the lineup on October 7, 2007, during a road game against the Washington Redskins, but was only able to get one catch for a few yards during the 34-3 loss.

After losing two of three games, Detroit was able to get into the bye week to allow some players to get some rest and recover from some injuries. The Lions would pick up another big win against the Tampa Bay Buccaneers, 23-16, on October 21, 2007. After Detroit's defense was able to force the Buccaneers to fumble at the Lions' seven-yard-line, Detroit was able to move the ball down the field which ended with an end around for Johnson to run 32 yards for the touchdown that helped secure the win in the fourth quarter[xxxix]. Johnson also had two receptions for 37 yards in the game. This was around the time that Johnson started to get some nicknames that would stick around him for a while.

His fellow receiver Williams called him "Megatron" during a story where he said that the Lions selected Johnson with the second draft pick for a reason. The nickname was because of how physically imposing he was when standing on the line of scrimmage, noting that his hands resembled that of a Decepticon from the Transformers movie that came out in 2007.[xl] Later on in the summer of 2008 after the season, Williams would also give the young receiver out of Georgia Tech, "Bolt. He's 6-5, and he's a 9.69 (second) guy."[xli] The fans often compared Johnson to Jamaica's Olympic sprinter Usain Bolt because they had similar height and running attributes.

The Lions would win back-to-back games over the Chicago Bears and the Denver Broncos, but would then lose seven of their last eight games to end the season with a 7-9 record. It was a positive step forward, but still disappointing considering the team started with a 6-2 record in the first half of the 2007 season. Johnson would finish the year having played in 15 games and had 48 receptions for 756 yards and four touchdowns. Johnson was considered the number-two wide receiving threat behind Roy Williams, who finished the year with 838 yards and five touchdowns.

At the conclusion of the 2007 season, fans started to learn that the injury Johnson suffered from the hit against the Eagles was a lingering injury that lasted for a majority of the season. It was a big part of why Johnson was usually either out to lunch, working out, or killing time in another part of the Lions' facility during the 45-minute period where reporters and members of the media were allowed to speak with players in the locker room.[xlii] It certainly explained why there were periods of the season where he was almost a non-factor and could not get open for receiving opportunities. Johnson also revealed that the pains in his lower back were so severe that he was often taking prescription medications to alleviate the pains so that he could take the field – which included taking Vicodin twice during each game. He would explain to media in the offseason that he probably tried to come back to the team too soon and did not allow himself to heal completely.

Considering the back injury, Johnson would publically state that he expected his sophomore year in the NFL to be a much bigger season after having the time to recover fully before the offseason workout program began. While he was not saying he could double the nearly 800 yards he had in his rookie season, he felt that the 1,200 he put up in the 14 games during his final year at Georgia Tech indicated that he would have no problem being able to have 1,000 receiving yards in his second season with the Detroit Lions. It was just a matter of the quarterbacks putting the ball in the air for him to go and get.

2008 Season

There was some promise for the Detroit Lions as they went undefeated in all four of their preseason games. But those games do not count, and the 2008 season for the Lions did not have as great of a start as the last year, starting with a 34-21 loss on the road against the Atlanta Falcons on September 7, 2008. As the Lions allowed Atlanta to run for more than 300 rushing yards, the Lions were seen arguing amongst each other along the sidelines.[xliii] It was Johnson's first NFL game in the state of Georgia and while he did not record a receiving touchdown, he had seven catches for 107 yards.

Johnson had one of his better games during in home game against the NFC North powerhouse Green Bay Packers on September 14, 2007. After the Packers gained a 21-0 lead through the middle of the second quarter, the Lions started to crawl slowly back and had two key touchdown passes to Johnson to give Detroit a brief one-point lead.[xliv] The first came on a 38-yard touchdown pass from Kitna early in the third quarter. Moments after Detroit forced a safety, Kitna completed a deep 47-yard pass to Johnson for the 25-24 lead. Both touchdowns were over the middle of the field where Johnson was able to outrun the Packers' secondary players. It looked like Detroit was going to gain the upset win after Johnson would finish with 129 yards on six receptions. But Kitna threw two untimely interceptions which were returned for touchdowns by Green Bay's Charles Woodson and Nick Collins as Green Bay won 48-25.

The losses continued to pile up as Johnson would struggle to follow up on his memorable performance against Green Bay. He had just four receptions for 40 yards during a 31-13 loss to the San Francisco 49ers on September 21, 2008. After a quick bye week, Johnson could only get two receptions of eight yards each in the 34-7 loss at home to the Chicago Bears. He would begin to bounce back on October 12, 2008, where he had four receptions for 85 yards and a 12-yard touchdown pass from Dan Orlovsky, filling in for an injured Kitna. In the fourth quarter, the Lions were driving down the field, and Orlovsky connected with Johnson on a deep 37-yard play that would have put Detroit in a position to add to their lead. However, Viking defenders Darren Sharper and Ben Leber hit Johnson to knock the ball loose for a fumble that Minnesota recovered. While video evidence showed he was down, the referees upheld the rule, and the Vikings took the momentum of that play to set up a game-winning field goal of 26 yards from Ryan Longwell to give Minnesota the 12-10 win.[xlv]

While the loss was questionable, the Detroit Lions looked like they were going nowhere. They had begun the season with five terrible losses and not a lot of positives to look forward to moving ahead. Just days before the trade deadline, the Lions decided to build up their stock in draft picks and traded away their top receiver in Roy Williams to the Dallas Cowboys, which provided the Lions with selections in the first, third and seventh round during the 2009 NFL Draft.[xlvi] This provided a huge opportunity for Johnson, who found himself becoming the number one receiver for the Lions' offense.

During their next game on the road in Houston on October 19, 2008, the Texans jumped ahead with a 21-point lead with an offense led by Matt Schaub and receivers like Owen Daniels, Steve Slaton, and Andre Johnson. Detroit would come back in the second half as the two teams exchanged touchdowns before a fourth quarter where the Lions fell short. Starting from their own four-yard line, Orlovsky was able to find Johnson open for a 96-yard touchdown pass that would be the fourth-longest touchdown pass in team history and the longest the Lions ever had since the 1998 season.[xlvii] Johnson finished with 154 yards, mostly from that one touchdown and then another reception for 58 yards. But Houston would hold on for the 28-21 win that kept Detroit winless.

Johnson would get plenty of opportunities for big games, but the Lions struggled as they continued to lose and even signed veteran Daunte Culpepper to a one-year contract in an effort to avoid a winless season. But Detroit continued to lose, despite Johnson being able to put up big numbers. In the 31-21 loss to the Indianapolis Colts on December 14, 2008, Johnson had nine receptions for 110 yards and one touchdown. The season ended during a 31-21 loss at Green Bay on December 28, 2008, where Johnson had nine catches for another 102 yards and two touchdowns. With the loss at Lambeau Field in Green Bay, Wisconsin, the

Lions became the only NFL team to have ever finished the regular season with a record of 0-16. At the end of the broadcast, Lions play-by-play announcer Dan Miller commented that by the record, Detroit was the worst team in NFL history and the numbers zero and 16 would forever be associated with the franchise. Before the 2008 season, the (dis)honor of the worst team in franchise history belonged to the Tampa Bay Buccaneers, who went 0-14 in 1976, then started the 1977 season with 12 straight losses.

Detroit had five different quarterbacks, so it made Johnson's overall season that much more impressive considering the inconsistencies around him. Johnson started all 16 games and finished with 1,331 yards and 12 touchdowns on 78 receptions. The Detroit offense only had 18 passing touchdowns, which was just another example of how much the Lions offense suffered overall. Despite how good his numbers were, Johnson would not be invited to the NFL's annual Pro Bowl game where the league's best played in an AFC vs NFC exhibition. The belief was that the 0-16 record for Detroit took away the value of anything that Johnson did.[xlviii] Changes were expected, and they were not just on the field, head coach Rod Marinelli was fired at the end of the season, along with most of the team's coaching staff. The firings actually started earlier in the year when Matt Millen, who faced years of criticism as the team's president and chief executive officer, was terminated on September 24, 2008.

2009 Season

Detroit's new general manager and chief executive officer Martin Mayhew was bringing in Jim Schwartz as the new head coach, who had a successful run as the defensive coordinator for the Tennessee Titans. Schwartz made some significant changes regarding the Lions' game plans for both sides of the ball, and it started with bringing in new assistant coaches that supported his philosophy. It was a standard change that happens for a team that changes head coaches in addition to front office staff members. The Lions also found themselves with the top draft pick in hand for the 2009 NFL Draft and they had an excellent list of options to choose from with a variety of quarterbacks, offensive tackles, and defensive linebackers. Considering that there were five different players to be taking snaps as starting quarterbacks for the Detroit Lions in the 2008 season, Detroit decided to go the route of a quarterback with Georgia's Matthew Stafford.[xlix]

Stafford garnered plenty of attention after his junior season saw him complete 61.4 percent of his throws for 3,459 yards and 25 touchdowns against just ten interceptions that included a three-touchdown performance to help the Bulldogs defeat the Michigan State Spartans in the 2009 Citrus Bowl[l]. Considering that he was someone that annually played the Georgia Tech Yellow Jackets, Johnson knew who he was, and it was great news for the receiver entering his third season in the NFL. Despite Johnson still being young in his NFL career, he was going to be someone who would need to build a working relationship with the new Lions quarterback; someone who entered a team with fans hoping for positive results and yearning for success. Johnson walked a line similar to the one that Stafford was about to embark on in 2009, so Johnson was going to be expected to help make the transition from college to professional football a little bit easier, even if there was a rivalry between Stafford's Georgia Bulldogs and Johnson's Georgia Tech Yellow Jackets. That did not mean the 2009 season was going to be an immediate turnaround from the 2008 season. The Lions were going to win more than zero games, but they were going to still face a few challenges as a team trying to find their consistency in performing like a well-oiled machine.

The losing streak would continue with a 45-27 loss visiting the New Orleans Saints on September 13, 2009, where Stafford was able to connect with Johnson on three receptions for a total of 90 yards that included a 64-yard pass play. But Stafford finished the day with 16 of 37 completions for 205 yards with three interceptions, all while New Orleans' Drew Brees threw for 358 yards and six touchdowns. Detroit would then lose at home during an NFC North game against the Minnesota Vikings, 27-13, where Stafford was able to connect with Johnson on their first touchdown together. It was an eight-yard pass in the second quarter that helped give the Lions a 10-0 lead before the Vikings were able to outscore Detroit 20-3 in the second half.

But a losing streak that had reached 19 games dating back to December 2007 finally came to an end when the Detroit Lions were able to defeat the Washington Redskins at home on September 27, 2009. Johnson had five receptions for 49 yards with Stafford completing 21 out of 36 of his passes for 241 yards and a touchdown to help Detroit take the 19-14 win[li]. Detroit Lions owner William Clay Ford made a public comment to the media that the win felt like getting a monkey off their backs that felt more like King Kong. He also said he hoped it was the beginning of building a winning culture in Detroit. Unfortunately, the Lions were still trying to find themselves as a unit.

The Lions tried to start on a positive note during a road game in Chicago on October 4, 2009, where Stafford was able to complete a deep catch and run to Johnson on the very first play of the match. The two would connect a total of eight times for a total of 133 yards. Detroit also scored three touchdowns in the first half before having nothing in the second half as Chicago won 48-24. Stafford would suffer a right knee injury that would affect him for the next few games, including a home game against the Pittsburgh

Steelers on October 11, 2009. If that were not bad enough for Detroit, Johnson would leave the game after a two-yard reception and would be hobbling on the sideline as he tried walking for the rest of the match. This led to Johnson not being available for their October 18, 2009, game at Green Bay (they lost 26-0) and then for the home game against the St. Louis Rams on November 1, 2009 (17-10 loss). Johnson would return for limited action on November 8, 2009, where he had two catches for 27 yards in a 32-20 loss. Those numbers would increase to eight receptions for 84 yards on the road at Minnesota during a 27-10 loss on November 15, 2009.

Things were looking grim for the season despite knowing they were not going to repeat the history they set in 2008 with a winless season. Detroit would have a chance to earn a memorable win at home against the Cleveland Browns, 38-37, on November 22, 2009. Johnson was the top receiver for the Lions with seven catches for 161 yards that included a 75-yard touchdown pass in the second quarter where the man known as Megatron would get past cornerback Brodney Pool with a double-move to get open for the catch and run into the end zone. Stafford was the star for the Lions as he led a late touchdown drive that ended with a one-yard pass to Brandon Pettigrew for the win, making him the first quarterback to have five touchdown passes in a game since Ray Buivid of the Chicago Bears accomplished that feat in 1937.[lii]

That one-game winning streak would last until Thanksgiving Day on November 26, 2009, before the visiting Green Bay Packers topped the Lions 34-12. The game started off looking like Detroit was going to have a chance to build off their win over Cleveland after they forced Green Bay to fumble on the opening kickoff, which led to a one-yard touchdown from Stafford to Johnson. But the Packers would score 27 unanswered points before the Lions had a safety and a field goal in the fourth quarter.

Detroit would have several games where they started high but fell flat by the end of the match. A great example took place on December 6, 2009, in Cincinnati, with Stafford completing a 54-yard touchdown pass in the early first quarter as Megatron would finish the game with six catches for 123 yard. However, Stafford struggled overall with just

11 completions after 26 attempts for 143 yards and threw two interceptions; one was returned by the Bengals' lineman Jonathan Fanene 45 yards for a touchdown as the home team would get the 23-13 win. Stafford would continue to suffer several injuries throughout the last few weeks of the season as they would lose their final four games to finish 2009 with a 2-14 record. It was a slight improvement considering their historical lack of wins the year before. Johnson still had some big numbers despite missing a few games and dealing with the right knee injury early in the season. Johnson finished 2009 with 67 catches for 984 yards and five touchdowns. It might not have been his best season, but considering all of the changes between the coaching staff, front office, and having a new quarterback to establish a professional relationship with, those numbers were still pretty impressive. There was also a lot more hope after the 2009 season than at the conclusion of the 2008 season.

2010 Season

Sometimes the greatest test of a player's character is when they are faced with a controversial moment in sports.

Detroit was on the road in Chicago for the season-opener on September 12, 2010, with the Lions on the move against the Bears defense that had always been considered one of the top 10 groups in the league for years. It was not the best of circumstances with Stafford leaving the game with a shoulder injury and Shaun Hill having to take over in the second half where the Bears scored on a fourth-quarter touchdown pass from Jay Cutler to Matt Forte for the lead. With 31 seconds left in the game and the Lions at the Bears 25-yard-line, Hill threw a jump ball to Johnson, who was able to get above Chicago's Zackary Bowman.

Both feet were down and inside the end zone without going out of bounds before he would roll over and let go of the ball. Detroit's sideline erupted, and Johnson was celebrating until the head official Gene Steratore announced to the fans that a catch can only be ruled complete if the receiver has possession of the football for the entire process of the catch; that means not letting go of the ball at all. Detroit was unable to complete their next passing attempts, and they would lose in Chicago, 19-14.[liii] It was the team's 21st straight loss on the road and a continuation of a common theme – "Lions lose, again." The team would not make excuses for the loss as the head coach Jim Schwartz said that if he was ever in a position where he blamed the referees for a loss, then it was time for him to no longer be a head coach in the NFL.

But this loss hurt because it was arguably a catch, and has since begun one of the most debated topics in NFL history – what is a catch? The controversy pops up often in games today, and there seems to be a lot of contradiction between the cases. Johnson's catch that was waived off in 2010 has since become a precedent. The one thing people wondered is how well the Lions would react the very next week as they hosted the Philadelphia Eagles at home on September 19, 2010. It was a shootout between the Eagles and Lions as Hill had a much better game with 335 passing yards and two touchdowns, one of them a 19-yard pass to Johnson late in the fourth quarter. However, Philadelphia included two touchdown throws by Michael Vick and three more ran in by LeSean McCoy to defeat the Eagles 35-32. It was a game where Detroit had a furious comeback, but fell short. Center Dominic Raiola commented that the team could not wait until the end of a game to score points if they wanted to win.[liv]

Detroit would continue to lose their next two games, including a 24-10 defeat by the Minnesota Vikings where Johnson had just 56 receiving yards and a close 28-26 loss visiting the Green Bay Packers on October 3, 2010. Johnson caught a 23 and 21-yard touchdown pass during the second quarter to keep the Lions close against Green Bay. But after Charles Woodson returned one of Hill's interceptions for a 45-yard touchdown, the Lions could only get field goals for the close loss. Johnson finished with 86 yards on six receptions.

Detroit would get their first win of the season at home against the St. Louis Rams on October 10, 2010, where Johnson had four catches for 54 yards and a one-yard touchdown during a 44-6 rout of the Rams. It was a better result than the next week when Detroit loss on the road against the New York Giants, 28-20, on October 17, 2010 despite Johnson have 146 yards on just five catches, including a deep 87-yard touchdown pass from Drew Stanton, who took over for an injured Hill. The Lions would go into the bye week having a 1-5 record. The good news coming back home on October 31, 2010, was that Stafford would be back as the quarterback, and that was even better news for Johnson.

In their first game together since the controversial loss to Chicago, they quickly connected on a 13-yard pass in the second quarter. After leading by just one point after the third quarter, Stafford would find Johnson in the end zone two more times in the fourth quarter for seven and 10 yards. A 17-yard fumble return by defensive tackle Ndamukong Suh would clinch the 37-25 win. Everything felt great about the game, but the Lions were not able to maintain the momentum as they would lose their next five games, even though Johnson would still be able to contribute with 10 catches for 128 yards and a touchdown in the 14-12 loss to Buffalo on November 14, 2010. Déjà vu was striking again for Detroit fans, and they started to lose hope, even thinking about who the team would consider drafting at the upcoming draft with a likely number-one selection again.

The defense would play even tougher in the final four weeks of the season that featured a 7-3 win at home over the Packers on December 12, 2010; granted Green Bay was without quarterback Aaron Rodgers for a portion of the game and Johnson had just one catch for 44 yards in a low-scoring affair. Johnson would bounce back with 152 yards on ten receptions to help the Lions earn a consecutive victory, 23-20, over the Tampa Bay Buccaneers on December 19, 2010. Straight wins were something the Lions had not done since the 2007 season when they finished 7-9 during Johnson's rookie season.

Detroit's defense was able to get two interceptions as part of a 17-point run to help defeat the Miami Dolphins 34-27 on December 26, 2010. Johnson had four receptions for 54 yards but sat out for the entire fourth quarter due to him aggravating an ankle injury that had been bothering him for the season[lv]. While his health status was announced day-to-day by Schwartz, he was not suited up for the season-finale on January 2, 2011, when the Lions defeated Minnesota at home, 20-13.

As Detroit finished the season a 6-10 record, Johnson had 77 receptions for the year with 1,120 yards and 12 touchdowns, which led the NFC. The performance was good enough for him to receive his first nod to the NFL's annual Pro Bowl game where he was a member of the NFC's all-stars. He only had one catch in the game for 11 yards as the NFC lost to the AFC, 55-41. Johnson's honors for the 2010 season also included being selected to the NFL's All-Pro second team and was given the Media-Friendly Good Guy Award among all of the Lions that season by both the Detroit Sports Broadcasters Association and the local chapter of the Pro Football Writers Association. If there was one thing correct about Johnson in his time in the NFL, it was that he was never considered disrespectful towards the media and attempted to make himself available as much as possible, a quality that is not often found across professional sports. Then again, Detroit had a lot of reasons to be happy considering that they were winning games more often than the previous two seasons.

2011 Season

Maybe there was something about the momentum of winning the final four games of the 2010 season that gave Lions some confidence entering the 2011 season. Johnson would have his best season at the time that began with helping the Lions win their first season opener since 2007 with a 27-20 win at Tampa Bay. It was a game where Stafford felt great with 305 passing yards and three touchdowns in the match where the team finally felt they were on their way to breaking 10 years of futility that included the 2008 winless season.[lvi] Johnson had six receptions for 88 yards that included a 36-yard touchdown from Stafford in the second quarter to give Detroit the lead. The two connected again for a one-yard touchdown as insurance for the victory.

The 2011 Detroit Lions showed that they were a much better team overall, proving they didn't have to throw the ball to just Johnson. Although Johnson would take advantage of his opportunities as he had two touchdowns that highlighted his three catch, 29-yard performance during their 48-3 dominant win over the Kansas City Chiefs. This was followed by a 108-yard performance on seven receptions with two touchdowns in a 26-23 win over the Minnesota Vikings. But the biggest highlight early in Detroit's successful season was on October 2, 2011, on the road against the Dallas Cowboys – granted, Dallas defensive coordinator Rob Ryan made a comment that Johnson would probably be only good enough to be the number three receiver in Dallas[lvii].

Detroit was trailing by 20 points at the halftime before Stafford was able to connect with Johnson for a big rally that led to Detroit getting the 34-30 win. Among his eight receptions for 96 yards, Johnson's big highlight came on a 23-yard touchdown in the end zone where Johnson kept over three Dallas defenders to make the catch in the fourth quarter. Johnson would snag a two-yard touchdown from Stafford despite Dallas having too many men on the field. It was as if the Cowboys had no answer for the man known by millions as the NFL's Megatron. The win in Dallas tied Johnson with Pro Football Hall of Fame receiver Cris Carter for having four straight games with two touchdown receptions.

The winning streak continued during a home game against the division rival Bears with a 24-13 win on October 10, 2011. Johnson had five catches for 130 yards that featured a 73-yard touchdown pass from Stafford. Detroit started the season 5-0, but would lose two close games against the

San Francisco 49ers, 25-19, on October 16, 2011, and then to the Atlanta Falcons, 23-16, on October 23, 2011. Johnson did have a 57-yard touchdown catch late in the third quarter, but Stafford struggled to find receivers against the Falcons defense, completing just 15 out of 32 for 183 yards.

Just before the bye week that was conveniently placed in the middle of the season, Detroit went on the road to Denver and took care of business against a struggling Broncos team, 45-10, on October 30, 2011. It was an offensive explosion with Stafford having 267 yards and three touchdowns through the air and the Lions rushing for 113 yards and one more touchdown on the ground. Johnson's 56-yard touchdown catch in the third quarter made him only the second wide receiver since 1970 to have 11 touchdown receptions in the first eight games of a single season; Randy Moss was the first[lviii]. The defense also scored points in the match as cornerback Chris Houston had a 100-yard interception of Tim Tebow for a touchdown. Defensive end Cliff Avril also had a sack, strip, and scoop for a 24-yard touchdown that was part of a 45-point run after Denver took a very early 3-0 lead.

There was a stretch of games where Johnson was averaging closer to 75 yards per game after that bye week break, but the Lions were trying to compete with the Green Bay Packers who were on a dominant roll as the highest scoring offense in the NFL with 560 points on the season. The first time the two teams met, Johnson was held to only 49 yards and one touchdown as Detroit lost at home, 27-15, on November 24, 2011. This was at a time of the season when the Lions had lost three of their four games coming out of the bye week and were fighting to keep their playoff hopes alive. They were able to bounce back with a 34-28 win over the Minnesota Vikings on December 11, 2011. Johnson had only 29 yards on three receptions, but he would be a big part of how the Lions finally broke their streak of missing the playoffs.

But there was nearly a road bump from an unexpected struggle during a road game in Oakland as the Raiders were able to hold a 27-14 lead into the fourth quarter. But Stafford led two late touchdown drives in the final five minutes – including a three-yard touchdown pass to Titus Young and a six-yard touchdown to Johnson – for the 28-27 win on December 18, 2011[lix]. Johnson, who also had a 51-yard touchdown drive, was an essential part of Detroit's offense as he finished the game with 214 yards on only nine receptions, including some key plays on the 98-yard game-winning drive that was capped by his second touchdown of the match.

The momentum continued as the Lions were able to clinch the franchise's first playoff berth since the 1999 season after they defeated the San Diego Chargers at home 38-10 on December 24, 2011. This was followed by Stafford leading a parade around the perimeter of the stadium as the players had their victory lap that included high-fives with fans who had been patiently waiting for a reason to be proud of their blue and silver attire. They chanted "playoffs" for the final minutes of the game and the moments afterwards.[lx] Johnson was one of three touchdown recipients from Stafford in the first round – a 14-yarder only seconds before the end of the first half –

which was the big play out of his four catches for 102 yards.

With the playoffs in hand and the Packers having already won the NFC North, Detroit was hoping to earn some pride and continue their momentum on the road in Green Bay on January 1, 2012. However, backup quarterback Matt Flynn set franchise records for the Packers with 480 passing yards and six touchdowns in the 45-41 win. Johnson had a career game of his own as he collected 11 catches for 244 yards and a touchdown, which came on a 13-yard pass from Stafford in the second quarter. The loss did not hurt the newfound optimism fans had in Detroit. However, they would find themselves having to go up against the New Orleans Saints – the NFC South Champions who finished 13-3 and were always one of the best offensive groups in the league behind quarterback Drew Brees.

The Saints quarterback was relentless against the struggling Lions secondary as he had 466 yards and three touchdowns in a 45-28 win on January 8, 2012, in the NFC Wild Card Round of the NFL playoffs.[lxi] Johnson did just about everything you could ask from an All-Pro wide receiver as he finished with 12 catches for 211 yards and two touchdowns; Johnson even helped provide a key block during Stafford's one-yard bootleg run to bring the game closer to a 24-21 deficit in the third quarter. But Saints' cornerback Jabari Greer helped clinch the playoff win with two interceptions in the fourth quarter.

Johnson's 214 yards against New Orleans was a franchise record for playoff performances, which quickly topped the 150 yards that both Brett Perriman and Leonard Thompson held back in the Detroit record books. Despite the early exit from the NFL playoffs, fans had a lot of reasons to be excited after the team finished 10-6 and were a distant second from the NFC North Division crown; Green Bay finished with a 15-1 record. Johnson set career highs with nearly 100 receptions for 1,681 yards and 16 touchdowns. He was once again invited to the NFL Pro Bowl that year while also leading the NFL in receiving yards and touchdowns to earn his first spot on the NFL's All-Pro first team.

However, Johnson was not very happy with the loss, even though he recognized in postgame interviews that making the playoffs was certainly a huge accomplishment for the team after years of the franchise not playing beyond the regular season. "We have some things to work on and we will," Johnson commented. "We know what we have to do to make the next step."

2012 Season

During the offseason, the Detroit Lions wanted to sign their star wide receiver to a larger contract so that they could have him under contract for a long-term period of time. Just a few months after the end of the 2011 season, Johnson signed an eight-year extension that was worth more than $130 million; $60 million was 100 percent guaranteed, which would make him the highest paid wide receiver in the NFL. Additionally, Johnson was also announced as the cover athlete for the new video game, Madden NFL 13.[lxii]

Detroit started the season off well with a win at home against the St. Louis Rams, 27-23, on September 9, 2012. Johnson finished the game with six catches for 111 yards while Stafford was able to bounce back after throwing three interceptions in the match to finish with 355 yards and had support from a young Kevin Smith to give Detroit the win. But the Lions would lose their next three games as the Lions fell to 1-3 before the bye week. However, Johnson was still making big contributions and piling up the statistics, which included 164 yards and one touchdown on ten receptions during a close 44-41 loss at Tennessee on September 23, 2012.

Johnson would continue to be a factor for the Lions success after the bye week that started with a 26-23 win in Philadelphia on October 14, 2012 where he had 135 yards on six receptions. A few weeks later, he had seven catches for 129 yards during their road win at Jacksonville, 31-14, on November 4, 2012, to give them three out of four wins after the week off. However, Detroit would not be able to replicate the success they had in 2011. In fact, they would lose their last eight games that more resembled the Lions from 2008 and 2009. However, Johnson would still make history, not just within the Lions franchise, but in NFL record books.

Adrian Peterson ran over the Detroit defense for 171 yards and a 61-yard touchdown as the Vikings defeated the Lions,

34-24 on October 28, 2012. But Johnson had a big game of his own with 12 receptions for 207 yards and an 11-yard touchdown catch late in the match to bring the Lions closer to the win. But on Detroit's final offensive drive, Johnson fumbled the ball steps after a catch that gave Minnesota the ball back to kill the clock.[lxiii] Johnson's momentum would continue with another 143 yards on five receptions during a 24-20 loss at Green Bay on November 18, 2012, but Stafford would turn the ball over on two costly turnovers in the final minutes as the Lions were unable to complete the comeback[lxiv]. On November 22, 2012, Johnson would add another 140 yards versus Houston in a 34-31 loss for the team's annual Thanksgiving Day game.

Johnson would have another big game with 13 catches for 171 yards that included a 46-yard touchdown in the third quarter to extend Detroit's lead, but the Lions were unable to hold the lead as Andrew Luck would lead back-to-back touchdown drives to give the Indianapolis Colts the 35-33 win. This proved once again that the Lions were not destined to repeat their 2011 success that included a playoff berth.[lxv] Bruce Arian, who was the interim head coach for the Colts at the time, had the line that said it best for both teams – "Some teams find ways to win. Others don't." It may have been a little bit of luck as well, which the Lions did not seem to have any of in the 2012 season.

During the last half of the season, Johnson was able to have consecutive games with at least 125 yards per game, which was a record that was formerly held by Pat Studstill. One of the biggest games was the home game against the Atlanta Falcons on December 22, 2012, in a game where Johnson would put himself into the league record books after having 11 catches for 225 yards; granted the Lions would lose 31-18. But the game was a huge win overall for Johnson as he was able to break the record for having the most receiving yards in a season that was once held by Jerry Rice (1,848 yards in 1995).[lxvi] The record was broken when Johnson caught a 26-yard pass from Stafford in the final quarter of the game, giving him 1,892 yards as he entered the final game of the regular season with what was seemingly a good chance to be the first wide receiver to have 2,000 yards in a single season. In addition to breaking Rice's single-season receiving record, Johnson also tied former Cowboys' receiver Michael Irvin's record for most 100-yard games in one season with 11 games.

With Detroit well out of a playoff hunt, fans were still tuning in to see the Lions host the Chicago Bears on December 30, 2012, for a chance to see if Johnson would hit 2,000 yards. It was a close game that came down to the wire as Stafford was having one of his better games with 272 yards and three touchdowns. But Johnson was only able to get five catches for 72 yards in the 26-24 loss to the Bears, which was just a tiny bit short of the 2,000-yard goal[lxvii]. But it was still another loss for the Lions who fell extremely short of their goals at the beginning of the season.

It was a disappointing season once again as the Lions were not able to carry the momentum from their 10-6 season in 2011, finishing 4-12 overall with eight-straight losses. Detroit tried to go with a passing offense and set a league record for the most passing attempts by a team in NFL history with 740; the Minnesota Vikings in 1981 had 701 behind quarterback Tommy Kramer.

Despite the team's struggles, Johnson finished with a total of 122 catches for 1,964 yards for an average of nearly 123 yards per game; which made him the first and only player in the NFL Super Bowl era that was able to average more than 120 yards per game in a single season. But that was not the original goal that Johnson and his teammates set out to do, even though it was a highlight of the negative season. Fans were once again frustrated with the Detroit Lions, who would extend their streak of not winning a playoff game to 21 years.

2013 Season

It was the final season for Schwartz's contract as the head coach of the Detroit Lions, so there was some extra pressure to bounce back after the disappointing 4-12 season in 2012 – especially since the team had been to the playoffs the year before. The Lions were able to have a big win during the season-opening home game against the Minnesota Vikings, 34-24, on September 8, 2013, thanks to big plays from newcomer Reggie Bush, who caught a short pass that he turned into a 77-yard touchdown. Johnson had four receptions for 37 yards in the game.

He would be a bigger factor in the road game against the Arizona Cardinals on September 15, 2013. Johnson was able to connect with Stafford on the main touchdown plays in the second quarter for the early 14-10 lead, starting with a 72-yard pass on the team's first drive and then a three-yard pass that capped off a 10-play, 92-yard drive. Detroit even had a 66-yard interception from DeAndre Levy, but the Cardinals were able to score nine points in the fourth quarter that included a one-yard touchdown from Rashard Mendenhall for Arizona to get the 25-21 win.[lxviii]

Detroit's offense was able to bounce back one week later against the Washington Redskins on September 22, 2013, where Johnson finished with seven receptions for 115 yards and one touchdown in a 27-20 win. Washington had a few mistakes that included two costly turnovers in the fourth quarter, and a play similar to Johnson's ruled no catch three years prior. Washington's Aldrick Robinson had a potential game-winning touchdown catch in the end zone which was ruled as incomplete because of a process similar to Johnson in 2010 against the Bears. It was initially ruled a touchdown before a review showed the ball came loose after he caught it.[lxix] It was a historic win for the Lions, who had not won a road game in Washington, D.C. since 1939; a streak that was the second longest in NFL history at the time. The Lions would win their next game at home against the Chicago Bears, 40-32, with Johnson having another two-yard touchdown to highlight a four receptions in a 44-yard performance.

Detroit would have their short winning streak snapped in Green Bay the very next week on October 6, 2013, with the Packers having a dominant 22-9 win; Johnson was unavailable due to a knee injury that happened in the game against the Bears. It also affected his time he spent on the field in the game on the road against the Cleveland Browns where Johnson only had three catches for 25 yards while the Lions were able to get the 31-17 win against the Browns. Maybe the time off helped Johnson because he started to hit his stride back at Ford Field for a home game against the Cincinnati Bengals on October 20, 2013. Between Detroit's Stafford and Cincinnati's Andy Dalton, the two quarterbacks combined for more than 700 passing yards where Johnson and A.J. Green each had 155 yards during the game. Johnson had a few more attempts that were close calls in the first half. But he snagged a 27-yard catch, spinning to grab the ball thrown behind him and then turned around to fall into the end zone for the first touchdown. In the next quarter, Johnson caught a 50-yard desperation throw from Stafford that he was able to grab above three Cincinnati defenders. But Mike Nugent was able to hit a last second 54-yard field goal to give the Bengals the 27-24 win.[lxx]

Considering all of the catch opportunities that Johnson was not able to come up with may not have set well with Detroit and Johnson, which probably gave Johnson some extra motivation in a home game against the Dallas Cowboys before the bye week on October 27, 2013. Stafford had another big game where he had 33 completions out of 48 throws for 488 yards and one touchdown, which came on a two-yard pass to Johnson on the team's first drive of the first quarter. But it was a back and forth game until Detroit's final drive. Stafford was able to get a key pass to Johnson for 22 yards to set up a 1-yard plunge by Stafford with 12 seconds left for the 31-30 win over the Cowboys. On the pass completion, Johnson ran a seam route where he was able to get behind the defender just enough for Stafford to throw a very quick bullet to his top receiver, who finished with 329 yards on 14 catches. The individual effort from Johnson was surprisingly not an NFL record as Flipper Anderson had 336 yards with the Los Angeles Rams during an overtime thriller against the New Orleans Saints back in November 1989.[lxxi]

The momentum continued after the one-week break on November 10, 2013, where Detroit was able to get a crucial 21-19 win over the Chicago Bears. Johnson finished the game with six catches for 83 yards and two touchdowns. The highlight if the game was a 14-yard catch in the corner of the end zone with a little more than two minutes left in the game that extended the Lions' lead to 21-13. The touchdown was Johnson's 63rd career goal in Detroit and broke the franchise record that was once held by Herman Moore.[lxxii] At this point in the season, Detroit found themselves at the top of the NFC North with a record of 6-3, which got fans excited again. However, the Lions would not be able to hold onto that division lead for long as they lost at Pittsburgh on November 17, 2013, despite Johnson leading the team with six catches for 179 yards, including a 79-yard touchdown in the 37-27 loss. Detroit then fell at home 24-21 to Tampa Bay on November 24, 2013. Johnson had another 115 yards on seven catches, but could not find himself with the ball in the end zone.

Detroit would have a chance to keep their playoff hopes alive by breaking their losing streak on Thanksgiving Day with a 40-10 win over Green Bay on November 28, 2013. The Lions scored 37 straight points in the rout which featured a 20-yard touchdown pass from Stafford in the third quarter. The win was significant not only because the Lions were still in the playoff hunt, but it was the first win on the holiday after nine straight losses; Detroit usually hosts a game on Thanksgiving every year.[lxxiii]

But the Lions would lose their final four games of the season, which involved them falling into third place in the NFC North after they lost a close 18-16 game at home to the Baltimore Ravens on December 16, 2013, a game where Johnson had 98 yards on six catches. But Justin Tucker kicked the game-winning field goal from 61 yards away. One week later, the Lions were unable to defeat the New York Giants as strong safety Will Hill had a 38-yard interception return to tie the game and force overtime where Josh Brown kicked the game-winning 45-yard field goal that would eliminate any chance Detroit had of going to the playoffs in the 2013 season.[lxxiv]

Giant would not play in the final game of the season because of a knee injury that was bothering him throughout the season, as Detroit would lose 14-13 at Minnesota on December 29, 2013. This gave Detroit the 7-9 record that had a lot of potential during the first half of the season before they would lose six of their last seven games to fall from first to nearly worst in the division. It was still a positive season for Johnson, even though the team was still unable to make the playoffs. Johnson finished the season with 84 receptions and finished just eight yards shy of 1,500 with 12 touchdowns. This allowed him to be invited to his fourth consecutive Pro Bowl, and he was selected for Team Deion Sanders in the first pro bowl that did away with the AFC vs. NFC rivalry and all-star teams drafted by legendary players as head coaches. But because of the knee injury, Johnson decided to decline to play and took the extra time to rest his body for the next season.

2014 Season

The offseason that led up to the 2014 season was somber, not only because of the decision that the team would not bring back Jim Schwartz as the head coach. Team owner William Clay Ford, Sr., passed away in March 2014 at the age of 88. This led the team to wear special patches on their jerseys for the entire season to honor the owner who passed away.[lxxv] His wife, Martha Ford, then became the new owner of the team. Another new addition to the Lions was head coach Jim Caldwell, who came to the team after his time with the Indianapolis Colts. This led to changes in how the offense and defense would prepare, and this paid dividends in the season opener.

During the 35-14 win over the New York Giants on September 8, 2014, on the primetime stage of Monday Night Football, Johnson continued to show why he was the best wide receiver in the NFL with seven catches for 164 yards with several plays where Johnson demonstrated that he could find a way to get open. During the opening drive for Detroit, Stafford scrambled to extend the play while Johnson was able to get past the New York secondary after a couple of Giants collided; this allowed Johnson to take a leisurely stroll for the 67-yard touchdown. Later in the quarter, Johnson was able to dive for a 16-yard touchdown pass towards the back of the end zone.[lxxvi] Johnson would have another 83 yards during the 24-7 loss at Carolina on September 14, 2014, and then another 82 yards during a 19-7 win while hosting the Packers on September 21, 2014. But Johnson would start to struggle with an ankle injury that kept him limited to just two catches for 12 yards during Detroit's 24-17 win on the road against the New York Jets on September 28, 2014.[lxxvii]

That ankle injury would affect Johnson's ability to contribute moving forward through the first half of the Lions' schedule. After having just one catch for seven yards during Detroit's 17-14 loss at home to the Buffalo Bills on October 5, 2014, Johnson was kept off active duty for the next three games so that he could heal up properly. The Lions were not going to risk their star wide receiver suffering a severe injury that could impact his overall longevity with the franchise. Detroit was all right during the three games that he had to miss as they were able to get three close yet pivotal wins that included a 24-23 win at home over the New Orleans Saints and a 22-21 win while visiting the Atlanta Falcons. But Johnson would be able to make his return to the team after the bye week and planned to make his return at full health and playing form during a 20-16 win over the Miami Dolphins on November 9, 2014. Johnson had seven catches for 113 and a 49-yard touchdown in the first quarter, but Stafford was able to get the comeback with a late 74-yard drive that ended with an 11-yard touchdown pass to running back Theo Riddick to clinch the game.[lxxviii]

Detroit would drop their next two games as the Arizona Cardinals (14-6), and the New England Patriots (34-9) held Johnson to under 60 receiving yards and away from the end zone. It was one thing for Johnson not to score a touchdown for a few games, but three straight games was a rarity that he was able to avoid during a 34-17 win while hosting the Chicago Bears on November 27, 2014, which gave Detroit back-to-back wins on the Thanksgiving holiday after losing nine in a row. Johnson was the star with 11 receptions for 146 yards and two touchdowns that helped Detroit come back from a 14-3 deficit after the first quarter.[lxxix] This was followed up by another excellent individual performance by Johnson during the Lions' 34-17 win at home over the Buccaneers on December 7, 2014. He had eight receptions for 158 yards and one touchdown catch.

Detroit would continue to win key NFC North division games towards the end of the season to help clinch a guaranteed playoff berth after the Lions defeated the Vikings at home, 16-14, on December 14, 2014, and then winning 20-14 at Chicago on December 21, 2014; a game where Johnson had six catches for 103 yards to lead all Detroit receivers. This would set up a game in Green Bay on December 28, 2014, that would decide the NFC North Division champion before going into the NFL playoffs. It looked like a perfect situation for the Lions because Green Bay quarterback Aaron Rodgers was entering the game with an injury to his left calf. Johnson was part of two scoring drives that included a 20-yard touchdown just before halftime, and then a four-yard touchdown catch early in the third quarter. But Rodgers led two long touchdown drives in the second half, followed by Stafford committing a penalty in the end zone to give Green Bay the safety as part of their 30-20 win for the divisional title in the final week of the regular season. It was a bitter pill for Detroit fans to swallow, but the bad taste left in their mouth after the loss went away since they knew their season was not over yet.

Detroit finished the year 11-5, and while they were second in the NFC North, they had still earned a wild card berth in the NFL playoffs, their first since the 2011 season and just their second in team history since the late 1990s. Detroit fans were obviously going to consider any chance of making the playoffs as a successful season and were hoping that they would finally have some luck on their side to get a win after the regular season. However, the Lions probably would have loved getting that Week 17 win over Green Bay to not only have the division championship, but likely a first-round bye and a home playoff game.

Instead, the Lions had to travel to Dallas to face the Cowboys in the NFC Wild Round playoffs on January 4, 2014. Johnson had five catches for 85 yards as part of Stafford's 323 yards and one touchdown as Detroit was leading 20-14 before the fourth quarter. Dallas quarterback Tony Romo was able to mount a comeback behind two touchdown drives, which led to Dallas winning the game after an 11-play drive that ended with an eight-yard pass to Terrance Williams for the Cowboys to earn the 24-20 win at home. It was unfortunately the Lions' eighth straight loss in the playoffs, which was tied with Kansas City for the longest postseason losing streak in league history.[lxxx]

Johnson would once again have a decent season that earned him a spot in the NFL's Pro Bowl, which he declined and instead took the time to heal up from several nagging injuries and would be replaced by wide receiver Allen Robinson of the Jacksonville Jaguars. But considering that Johnson had an ankle injury that cost him from appearing in three games and may as well have done the same in two additional games where he totaled three catches for 19 yards. He still finished with 71 receptions for 1,077 yards and eight touchdowns. It was a down year when compared to the past few seasons Johnson had, and he would miss being included in the NFL's All-Pro first team for the first time since 2009 and did not lead the NFC in receiving yards for the first time in that same period. Johnson probably would not have cared about any of that since he was now winless in his only two playoff appearances and was starting to get closer to that age in the NFL when players start to suffer declines in performance.

2015 Season

Unlike the previous season, the Detroit Lions did not get off to a hot start and would lose their first five games. Johnson did not reach the 100-yard mark in any of those games and had some struggles hitting his usual marks. The season-opener at San Diego on September 13, 2015, is an excellent example of his early season slump as he had just two receptions for 39 yards – most came on a 28-yard catch – during the Lions' 33-28 loss to the Chargers. He did bounce back for a respectable 83-yard, 10-catch game with one touchdown during a loss at Minnesota, 26-16, and then had another eight receptions for 77 yards in the 24-12 loss at home to the Denver Broncos.

Johnson would be at the wrong end of a controversial play once again, similar to the season-opening loss in Chicago back in 2010. During a Monday Night Football matchup on October 5, 2015, the Lions were marching down the field during the final two minutes of the game and looked like they were about to have a huge upset win over the Seattle Seahawks, who were coming off back-to-back appearances in the Super Bowl. Johnson caught a pass on a slant route and started to make his way into the end zone for what would have been an 11-yard touchdown for a potential 17-13 win. However, Seahawks defensive enforcer Kam Chancellor was able to come from behind Johnson and punch the football out of Johnson's hand just before the ball crossed the plain of the goal line. The controversy followed that linebacker K.J. Wright intentionally batted the ball to the back of the end zone, which should have given Detroit the ball on the one-yard line and about 1:46 left in the game – an excellent opportunity that the Lions would have surely been able to take advantage of for the win. The referees ruled it a touchback and Seattle was able to hold on for the 13-10 win at home, and another heartbreaking loss for Johnson. "It's unfortunate, but you can't put the game in the referee's hands," Johnson told the media.[lxxxi]

Johnson was able to set the franchise record in the very next game on October 11, 2015, with his 673rd reception of his career with the Detroit Lions – the highlight of Johnson's five receptions was for 67 yards to break the record once held by Herman Moore. However, the Lions were unable to get any consistent offense going during the 42-17 loss at home to the Arizona Cardinals.[lxxxii] Stafford attempted to get the ball to Johnson more, but often threw interceptions and the Lions had a total of six turnovers in that game, which led to Dan Orlovsky being brought in during the fourth quarter; the first time Stafford would be benched in his seven years in the NFL. Considering that Detroit was the last remaining winless team in the NFL, it marked the eighth time in franchise history that has happened, the most of any franchise in the league. That winless streak would be snapped during a home game against the Chicago Bears; it just was not that easy for Johnson and the Lions.

On October 18, 2015, Johnson was able to have a big game where he had six receptions for 166 yards and snagged a six-yard touchdown after a 66-yard drive that took only two minutes for a brief three-point lead late in the fourth quarter. However, Bears quarterback Jay Cutler threw deep to Marquess Wilson, who drew the pass interference to set up Robbie Gould's 29-yard field goal to send the game into overtime. Minutes into the overtime period, Stafford was able to complete a 51-yard pass to Johnson, who was covered only by Chicago's Harold Jones-Quartey, and single coverage never works on the man known as Megatron, which brought Detroit to Chicago's seven-yard-line. This allowed Matt Prater to hit the game-winning 27-yard field-goal for Detroit to be able to improve to 1-5. Johnson said in the post-game press conference that they were happy just to get a win, especially against a rival within the NFC North Division.[lxxxiii]

The Lions would continue to struggle again as they would drop their next two games. Just before the bye week,

Detroit faced the Kansas City in a match that was played at Wembley Stadium in London, England, as part of the NFL's annual International Series. Johnson would only have five catches for 85 yards, but he would once again reach another career milestone. He was able to become the player who reached 11,000 receiving yards faster than any other player in NFL history. It took Johnson 127 games in the league to hit the milestone after making a 17-yard catch in the second quarter of the 45-10 loss to Kansas City – a record once held by St. Louis Rams legend Torry Holt.[lxxxiv]

Detroit would win six of their last eight games of the season to finish with a 7-9 record and, once again, would miss the playoffs. Johnson did have a few highlight games, but was not able to play with the consistency that fans were familiar with in recent years. During a 45-14 win over the Philadelphia Eagles on November 26, 2015, Johnson had three touchdowns, including a 25-yard pass from Stafford – who had five touchdown passes in the game – to help the Lions have a total of 430 offensive yards in the match. Johnson had a few games where he barely missed even getting 20 yards. But in the final game of the season,

Johnson would have ten receptions and 137 yards during a 24-20 win in Chicago on January 3, 2016. Johnson had a touchdown where he was able to get behind the Bears' secondary for a 36-yard pass from Stafford into the left corner of the end zone. It was the sixth consecutive season that Detroit was able to leave the Windy City with a victory; part of that was the kinds of games that Chicago quarterback Cutler had with three interceptions thrown to the Detroit defense, including a deflection off rookie Cameron Meredith that fell softly into the hands of James Ihedigbo.

During the 2015 season, Johnson may not have had his best individual numbers, but they were still impressive enough to place him among the best playing in the league. He was able to catch a total of 88 passes for 1,214 yards and nine touchdowns, which helped him hit the 1,000 receiving yards mark for the sixth consecutive season and his seventh overall – tied for 12th all-time in the NFL. Johnson was just one season away from having another 1,000 yards to be in a tie for the fourth most with Hall of Fame receivers like Cris Carter, Randy Moss, Terrell

Owens, Steve Largent, Marvin Harrison, Isaac Bruce, and Torry Holt.[lxxxv]

People did not know until a few months later, but Johnson would be the wide receiver with the second-most catches in a final season behind only Sterling Sharpe, who had 94 catches in the 1994 season with the Green Bay Packers[lxxxvi]. However, that was a note in Johnson's career that was not noticed until he made a shocking announcement about his nine-year career with the NFL – it was over.

Chapter 5: Johnson's Retirement from the NFL

With the 2015 NFL season completed, many players retired in early 2016, including Peyton Manning, who had just won his second Super Bowl championship with the Denver Broncos. Other notable retirements included veteran cornerback Charles Woodson, defensive end Jared Allen, and running back Marshawn Lynch. But none surprised the world of football as much as the announcement of Calvin Johnson's departure from professional football.

Rumors started to swirl about Johnson's future in the NFL. The news came out in January that Johnson had told only a select group of family and friends that 2015 was his last year, including Lions head coach Jim Caldwell just one day after the team's 24-20 win in Chicago on January 3, 2016.[lxxxvii] The reports also noted that Caldwell asked for Johnson to take his time with the decision before making the final choice, and the Lions were hoping that their all-star wide receiver would possibly change his mind before filing the necessary paperwork to make it official with the league offices.

But the one thing that was certain in March 2016, and that was that he was planning on leaving football and retiring from the Detroit Lions after nine seasons in the NFL with more than 11,000 receiving yards and six invitations to the NFL's annual Pro Bowl. He also owned just about every record in his position for anyone who has ever played under the Detroit Lions organization.[lxxxviii] It was a fascinating way of retiring as Johnson said in a team-released statement that he was not going to have an official press conference announcing his retirement from professional football.

In the statement, Johnson also commented that it was a very lengthy discussion that involved many of the people closest to him, including his family, and came to a tough decision to leave the sport. He commented that he was not leaving football on bad terms with the game, the NFL, or with the Detroit Lions, which some might have jumped toward as a conclusion. Still, he gave his thanks to the people within the Lions' organization, as well as all of the individuals who had supported him in his mission to playing professional football – from his high school coaches to Georgia Tech and the people who brought him into the league and developed him into the athlete he would become.

The announcement came as a surprise to many with responses on social media by other great football players. Hall of Fame wide receiver Jerry Rice wrote on Twitter that he had respect for Johnson and called him an "outstanding" star in the league and an even greater human being. His quarterback Matthew Stafford also said in the team statement that Johnson was going to be someone who the rest of the team and the fan base in Detroit were going to miss very significantly. But part of why Johnson made the decision was because the big man – standing at six-foot-five and weighing just under 240 pounds – had sustained many injuries that still caused him problems. In the last four years in the NFL, Johnson had suffered from problems with his knees and fingers, as well as trying to play the last half of the 2015 season with an ankle injury. However, he was always able to play at a very high level as arguably one of the best to play in the NFL at the wide receiver position.

The talk about Johnson seriously contemplating retirement began in January 2016, with a lot of talk about why he would make the decision to leave millions of dollars with a future contract with the Lions. But early on, people were left to speculate the reasons why. For example, the injuries were one of the big reasons why ESPN.com staff writer Michael Rothstein wrote a column about Johnson's consideration of leaving the game.[lxxxix] Another reason for the retirement was the belief that it was Johnson's time, considering that it was once considered crazy for other players to leave the game young because of the injuries, a lack of interest, or possibly a combination of both. There is also a belief from Rothstein that the lack of winning probably had something to do with it since the Lions have missed the playoffs for seven of the nine seasons – losing both playoff games Johnson played in. Overall, Detroit has gone 54-90 during Johnson's career, and there have been some people who believed that the Lions were going to go into rebuilding mode, which is not necessarily a perfect situation for someone who would most likely be unable to enjoy a championship run with a franchise like the Lions.

Rothstein also commented that money was a discussion, with Johnson having a cap value of about $24 million for the 2016 season and was likely to make nearly $16 million. But he has made plenty of money over his NFL career, and rightfully so for one of the best wide receivers in NFL history. At the same time, the Lions were going to hire Bob Quinn as the new general manager[xc]. These new additions might have led to some of the new front office powers trying to convince Johnson to take a bit of a pay cut to reduce the amount of impact his contract would have on the team's overall salary cap. Regardless, it was a situation where neither party was really at fault. Johnson is someone who does not want to play if he feels it is not the best decision, and the Lions were not necessarily kicking him out of the team. Everyone left on good terms, but it did not mean that the news was any less shocking throughout not only the NFL but all professional sports.

Many NFL players were taking to social media about the retirement, including defensive cornerback Patrick

Peterson of the Arizona Cardinals, who stated that Johnson made him a better player on the field; anyone who has to regularly line up across from someone like Johnson has to play at their best[xci]. Hall of Famer Deion Sanders also commented about Johnson and Peyton Manning, who retired within a day of Johnson, saying that they were arguably two of the best players in NFL history. Others who often competed alongside him with the Lions or faced him were in agreement that Johnson was essentially a freak of nature athlete who will be remembered for what he was able to do to provide a legitimate offensive weapon for the Detroit Lions.

When the news came out, not everyone believed it was true. In fact, some of his teammates thought that it might have been a joke that Johnson was playing on them. He did make a mention of it in the early fall of what would be his ninth and final season in the NFL, but players like wide receiver Corey Fuller thought that Johnson was speaking in a more nonchalant, not-so-serious tone of voice.[xcii] While Fuller was attending a special appearance to help raise money for a weight room for the Detroit Police Athletic

League, he commented that when they talked about retirement, Johnson said there was a chance it was his final season. But the retirement talk was kept between Johnson and what Fuller described was a tiny group of people in the Detroit locker room. Even one month after the retirement announcement, Fuller noted that it had not fully hit him that Johnson's time with the Lions was over. It likely will hit him when players start reporting back to Lions headquarters for the spring workouts in April 2016.

The interesting thing about Johnson's retirement is that many compared it to another great Detroit Lion player – running back Barry Sanders. He was the man who was considered by many to be the greatest running back in NFL history and had retired a little abruptly at the end of the 1998 season after finishing just 1,457 yards short of the all-time rushing record, stating that he did not have the same drive to give everything he could to the game.[xciii] Back in the late 1990s, someone retiring at a younger age was a little bit of a shocking suggestion. But in 2016, there have been other players who are retiring despite many people feeling that they still have plenty left in the tank physically

– D'Brickashaw Ferguson retired at the age of 32 while A.J. Tarpley left the NFL at just 23 years old.

Sanders said recently that he was planning on having a sit-down discussion with Johnson to talk about possibly changing his mind. In a fashion similar to the Godfather, Sanders jokingly made the comment that he would make Johnson an offer that he could not refuse. The hope seems to be that Sanders is going to have a discussion with Johnson during the offseason and possibly find a way to help him maybe locate the passion for returning to football; maybe just in time for when the Detroit Lions are set to start pre-season training camp in July and August 2016. While the former Lions running back made some jokes about the situation, he did comment that it is becoming a bizarre sight to see so many players quitting professional football at an early age for personal reasons that go beyond injuries they have. Sanders knows how tough the decision is since he knows how tough it was for him back in 1998 – but maybe he can help explain to Johnson why he should think about possibly going back to Detroit and suiting up in the blue and silver in the fall of 2016.

Sanders is not the only former Detroit Lion who wants to urge Johnson to reconsider the decision to retire from professional football. Nate Burleson has a plan that Johnson take the year off from football in this "retirement" and then try to come out of retirement and find a way to sign with the New England Patriots to win a Super Bowl; he added that Johnson deserves to be able to do so[xciv]. It would not be something outside the realm of possibility because the Lions would have to be willing to pay his higher salary if he does come back, leaving the Lions with no choice but to cut him from the team. This would make Johnson a free agent who could sign with any team. There are also some players who think Johnson will come back before then, like Adam Jones of the Cincinnati Bengals, claiming that his retirement might only last six months.

As far as his head coach Jim Caldwell is concerned, Johnson made a smart decision that might have been considered a little bit foolish by many outside of the organization, including fans. While he admitted there were many emotions he felt when the announcement was made official, he commented that he was lucky to work with someone like Johnson. He was a great player and great competitor, but someone who has done plenty of things away from the field to stand out as a great overall person as well.[xcv] Caldwell commented that the decision to retire was what Johnson felt was the best decision for himself and for his family, which is all that matters since he looked at all of the available options moving forward and carefully weighed out the pros and cons for what he was about to do.

But the one thing that Johnson's retirement has started is the discussion of whether more key players in the league might follow suit as well. It has been a difficult time for the league as they continue to face criticisms over concussion protocols and research that has started to find links between behavioral and mental health problems with playing football for several years. One story from NESN.com comments that Johnson might be setting a precedent for players who could still perform leaving the game around the age of 30. This includes J.J. Watt, who recently announced that he plans on retiring when he feels he cannot play at the high level that he has been known for since coming to the Houston Texans.[xcvi] While he is not currently showing any signs of slowing down at age 27, Watt commented that he does not want to stay in football just for the sake of playing in the league. With how high-profile players like Johnson have left the game earlier than expected, it is going to be interesting how other players like Watt and some of the other big names in football might handle their futures in the NFL once they get to that age. It is a time when many injuries that have accumulated over the years start to add up to nagging pains that often stick around for the rest of their lives.

Chapter 6: How Johnson Compares to All-Time Greatest Receivers

At the age of 30, Johnson may have had some left in the tank as a professional athlete in the NFL. No one can deny that he did leave his mark as one of the best in league history as a dominant wide receiver. At the end of his nine seasons with the Detroit Lions, Johnson was able to catch a total of 731 passes for a total of 11,619 yards and 83 touchdowns against just about every defense in the NFL. Concerning all-time ranks in league history, Johnson is 27th in receiving yards and is 22nd in receiving touchdowns, but when you look at players in nine years playing in the NFL, Johnson has the third most behind Holt's 11,864 yards and Rice's 11,776 yards. Ever since he was selected by the Lions in the 2007 draft, no other player has come close to having more yards, touchdowns, or games with at least 100-yards than Megatron (46). He has also averaged the most yards per game in his career with 86.1 – nearly nine yards more than Holt, the closest anyone in league history has been to topping Johnson.

One of the things that made Johnson incredibly unique in the league is that there were not many receivers at his size that had even a margin of success playing past college. In fact, only six other players in league history since 2007 who were at least six-foot-five and weight the same as Johnson's 237 pounds had at least one touchdown in their careers. Five of those six players were only able to combine for 200 total receptions against Johnson's impressive 731. Johnson was a dominating player that was easily considered the best wide receiver in the NFL, though he was never able to win a playoff game. Usually, a team that has a player with Johnson's numbers would have at least one a few games after the regular season; many of them even have Super Bowl championship rings – i.e. Moss, Holt, and Bruce. Even players like Owens and Chad Johnson, who were usually on mediocre teams, were able to win some playoff games with their teams. It was a sad thing considering that there was a lot of hope when Detroit drafted the young Johnson out of Georgia Tech – especially with the amount of buzz he was able to create just by completing his pre-draft workout and the NFL Rookie Combine in 2007. For example, Johnson is considered the only player who was at least 6'5" with a 40-yard dash time that was under the 4.4-second mark – he ran those 40 yards in an impressive 4.35 seconds.

Johnson is not alone regarding retiring early as there was a trend with players deciding to leave professional football at age 30 or younger. About 24 percent of the players who retired from the NFL in 2011 were age 30 or older. Those numbers continued to climb to nearly 50 percent with players that included running back Marshawn Lynch, who left the Seattle Seahawks at the age of 29.

Chapter 7: Johnson's Charitable Work

Johnson has performed many good deeds that started well before he was lacing up his shoes for the Detroit Lions. During the summer of 2006, Johnson was still in the middle of his studies in management at Georgia Tech, which was accompanied with a little bit of a background in building construction. That summer, Johnson had a choice as to whether he would participate in the construction of luxury condominiums that were designed to be environmentally friendly, or he could be involved in a project that wanted to provide solar-powered latrines to help the overall sanitation in the smaller country of Bolivia.

Johnson would choose to go to Bolivia, and was able to be a part of a project that tackled an issue that billions throughout the world were dealing with – proper sanitation and not having clean toilets to use. In the school's newspaper, *The Technique*, Johnson spoke about the choice he made; he thought it would be more fun to help the people of Bolivia.[xcvii] It was a joint effort between George Tech and Emory University students working together to develop a plan, which Johnson was a big part of because of his background in management. The solar-powered latrines were completed rather quickly and were constructed using materials that were easy to get ahold of in Bolivia. Materials bike rubber, cement, and tin foil, which was used to create an efficient system to use energy from the sun to help provide a fully-functioning latrine for use. It also used the power to transform the waste into usable fertilizer for crops.

It was a real testament to the type of person that Johnson is because he was, at that point, a star college football player that could have gone the easy route and worked on luxury condos. Instead, he chose to do something that provided a necessity to people who would have otherwise had to settle for much less. He even commented to the school newspaper that putting in that type of work provides a chance to look at what life is like for another part of the world and how much work goes into having something that many people in first-world countries would likely take for granted, commenting that he has a larger appreciation for things that he does have. The work continued after the 2006 football season, and he even went back to Bolivia with the team in late January to help add more solar-powered latrines.

A few years later while still a young star in the National Football League, Johnson founded a charitable organization called the Calvin Johnson Jr. Foundation, Inc.; which has a goal of making sure that children who are at-risk can receive the dedicated education or training they need while also helping them develop socially.[xcviii] His foundation also works with other groups to help provide financial support for families as well. The mission statement on the organization's website says that the goal is to change the mindset of struggling to survive while also improving self-esteem. The charity provides opportunities for them to improve their thinking process and to set goals for themselves while feeling empowered to move towards their dreams, which is why the foundation has the motto, "Catching Dreams." Johnson still acts as the president of the executive board and the organization has achieved a lot since starting in 2008, which included providing scholarships and awards for more than 35 student-athletes since then. Nearly 30 of those students were part of the third annual Leadership Conference in 2014.

Johnson's foundation has also helped sponsor many toy drives that have been able to provide gifts and care packages to more than 200 children who were either homeless or children of parents who were incarcerated. They have also helped raise money for breast cancer awareness and treatment, as well as helping hundreds of children have access to being able to participate in football camps with NFL stars and other professional athletes – at no cost to their family. The focus is on providing the opportunities, and Johnson's foundation is providing children with those chances so that they can develop their skills to succeed down the road.

The organization has also grown to start providing role model awards, with William Mann III becoming the first recipient in March 2015; a student at Southwest Christian Academy in College Park, Georgia who plays basketball and football while also acting as an Eagle Scout that helps others succeed. It is just another way that Johnson provides to children who are hoping to make impacts in the world like Johnson has; especially showing that they can reach the heights captured by the man known best by football fans as Megatron – they just need the opportunity to get started by someone who has been there.

With the fact that Johnson retired from playing professional football in January 2016, there are some people who believe he is likely going to do a lot more with his foundation as he has told members of the media that he hopes to continue doing more with his foundation that is helping at-risk children and supportive organizations in the communities – maybe beyond the communities in Atlanta, Georgia and Detroit, Michigan that he has called home nearly his entire life[xcix]. He has even thought about going back to Georgia Tech to finish his education, which would probably allow him to learn more skills to continue working as a president of his current foundation and maybe some other business endeavors.

Chapter 8: Personal Life

One of the things that have continued to grow for Johnson is his Christian faith, which he wears on his sleeve. On his left arm, Johnson has a tattoo that shows the crucifixion of Jesus Christ and another that depicts a cross with a crown on the top, showing wings and sun rays that stretch up his shoulder and towards his neck displayed on his right arm – he drew the designs for both of his tattoos.[c] He also draws often, which is something that he started when he was in the sixth grade. One of the things he draws often are spiritual symbols and figure, which was mentioned in a YouTube video special through the NFL Players Association. He admits that his younger brother's art skills would put his to shame.

But his faith continues to be a big part of his life, both on and off the football field. While still playing in the NFL, Johnson was often known for leading regular Bible studies with teammates who also identified themselves as Christians. During an interview with FCA Magazine in 2012, he noted that being an athlete in the NFL provides a big stage to be able to spread God's Word[ci]. While he has never been known as a brash wide receiver like some of his peers (i.e. Terrell Owens and Chad "Ochocinco" Johnson), he does not mind being very vocal about his faith. He just lets his football abilities speak for themselves on the football field. Johnson is considered another positive Christian role model who found success in professional athletics and was able to reach out to people in that way. Other examples include Reggie White and Russell Wilson.

There have always been doubts about how serious some professional athletes are with things like their religious beliefs. But in 2013, Johnson started to show that he was willing to put his money where his mouth spoke concerning his faith. During a feature story from the New Republic called "The Drain Catcher" about how some athletes fall for get-rich-quick schemes which led to them falling into financial pitfalls after their playing days were done, there was a brief moment that showed Johnson doing something unique compared to his peers. The story focuses on Corey Galloway of Legacy Growth Partners, an organization that helps with investments and making sure professional athletes have a better financial future.

However, he also talked about some of the projects he has helped fellow athletes with, which includes Johnson, who is currently working on a film titled "Real Love." The plot of the movie focuses on a young girl who attempts to maintain her virginity to stay true to her Christian faith.[cii] Galloway mentions that the goal of the film for his firm is to get their money back while Johnson is more focused on getting a particular message based on his Christian faith across to the audience. Since the media stories in 2013, there have not been any stories about whether the film was scheduled to be released in theaters or become a straight-to-DVD movie.

But there is no denying that Johnson's faith has had something to do with the fact that he has done incredible work for his communities in Georgia and Michigan through the Calvin Johnson Jr. Foundation to help in the many different ways mentioned earlier. He told the media that giving back was built into his culture, and that the more people like him do it, the desire to do more increases, especially when seeing the long-lasting effects that programs like his foundation have created have for troubled youths.[ciii] His mother Arica Johnson, who serves as the vice president of the executive board of her son's foundation, said that being a Christian involves doing what God says in the Bible – giving back and helping others because it becomes cyclical. The people who are helped will then be more likely to continue helping others like them.

Based on that comment and the things that Johnson has done while playing football, there is a good chance that people can expect to see him decide to spend more time on his foundation and maybe a few more projects that will be focused around his Christian beliefs of helping others in need. He will have some free time, and we may finally be able to see the "Real Love" film that has been talked about for about three years, as of this writing.

Chapter 9: Johnson's Overall Legacy

After the news had broken about Johnson's surprising retirement from the NFL, Fox Sports writer Cameron DaSilva compiled a list of 10 "ridiculous" statistics about his career that could make a case about how he deserves to be considered a member of the Pro Football Hall of Fame in Canton, Ohio. Some argue that Johnson should be inducted on his first attempt on the voting ballot. One interesting statistic is that Johnson was the only player in the NFL's Super Bowl era to average 120 yards per game in a single season, which was in the historic 2012 season where he set the all-time single-season receiving record of 1,964. He also accounted for more than 30 percent of Stafford's career passing yards and more than 30 percent of Stafford's career touchdowns.[civ]

The one thing that any football fan would agree on is that Johnson was a rare breed of wide receiver who was playing at a higher level than nearly everyone else in the NFL. Even the stubborn fans from Chicago, Green Bay, and Minnesota may or may not have celebrated upon the news of Johnson's retirement. It is one thing to be fast or tall, but

Johnson was the one man who could combine both and still be able to put up the numbers that he was able to during those nine seasons. It is questionable if he would have been able to break the all-time receiving career record if he would have finished his contract with the Detroit Lions franchise. While no one could predict whether Johnson would have been able to play the 20 seasons that Jerry Rice was able to. But if Johnson would have continued to play for that long of a career, it is likely that he would have put up the numbers that would have probably broken Rice's 22,895 yards and nearly 200 touchdown receptions.

However, part of why Johnson decided to retire from the NFL was because of the numerous injuries that he suffered and because he was often being hit hard and trying to go up for passes in heavy defensive traffic. It is hard to imagine he would not have suffered at least one big knee or ankle injury that would have cost him a season like many great receivers have had to deal with.

Johnson will always be considered one of the best wide receivers to have ever played the game and was able to show it with his brief time in the league; just like another great Detroit Lion named Barry Sanders, who showed he was possibly the greatest running back in league history. Johnson stood out for what he was able to do, but he was also able to do so with teams that performed poorly and was able to be the mature leader who never complained about the hand the football gods dealt him. In the end, not only was Johnson one of the best receivers statistically, he was one of the best role models as well.

Final Word/About the Author

I was born and raised in Norwalk, Connecticut. Growing up, I could often be found spending many nights watching basketball, soccer, and football matches with my father in the family living room. I love sports and everything that sports can embody. I believe that sports are one of most genuine forms of competition, heart, and determination. I write my works to learn more about influential athletes in the hopes that from my writing, you the reader can walk away inspired to put in an equal if not greater amount of hard work and perseverance to pursue your goals. If you enjoyed *Calvin Johnson: The Inspiring Story of One of Football's Greatest Wide Receivers,* please leave a review! Also, you can read more of my works on *Colin Kaepernick, Aaron Rodgers, Peyton Manning, Tom Brady, Russell Wilson, Michael Jordan, LeBron James, Kyrie Irving, Klay Thompson, Stephen Curry, Kevin Durant, Russell Westbrook, Anthony Davis, Chris Paul, Blake Griffin, Kobe Bryant, Joakim Noah, Scottie Pippen, Carmelo Anthony, Kevin Love, Grant Hill, Tracy McGrady, Vince Carter, Patrick Ewing, Karl Malone,*

Tony Parker, Allen Iverson, Hakeem Olajuwon, Reggie Miller, Michael Carter-Williams, John Wall, James Harden, Tim Duncan, Steve Nash, Pau Gasol, Marc Gasol, Jimmy Butler, Dirk Nowitzki, Draymond Green, Pete Maravich, Kawhi Leonard, Dwyane Wade, Ray Allen and Paul George in the Kindle Store. If you love football, check out my website at claytongeoffreys.com to join my exclusive list where I let you know about my latest books and give you lots of goodies.

Like what you read? Please leave a review!

I write because I love sharing the stories of influential people like Calvin Johnson with fantastic readers like you. My readers inspire me to write more so please do not hesitate to let me know what you thought by leaving a review! If you love books on life, football, or productivity, check out my website at claytongeoffreys.com to join my exclusive list where I let you know about my latest books. Aside from being the first to hear about my latest releases, you can also download a free copy of *33 Life Lessons: Success Principles, Career Advice & Habits of Successful People*. See you there!

Clayton

References

[i] "Barry Sanders." *NFL.com*. National Football League. N.d. Web.
[ii] "Calvin Johnson Biography." *Jockbio.com*. Black Book Partners, LLC. N.d. Web.
[iii] Battista, Judy. "Johnson Has No Baggage and a Seat In First Class." NYTimes.com. New York Times. 6 April 2007. Web.
[iv] Wywrot, Chrissie. "Growing up in Tyrone, Ga., football wasn't Calvin Johnson's first sport." *DetroitLions.com*. Detroit Lions. 17 May 2012. Web.
[v] Glier, Ray. "Georgia Tech's star receiver just can't miss." *USAToday.com*. USA Today. 28 August 2006.
[vi] "Sandy Creek to retire Calvin Johnson's number." *AJC.com*. Atlanta-Journal Constitution. 22 October 2010.
[vii] Jordan, Jason. "What Calvin Johnson was like in high school" *USATodayHSS.com*. USA Today. 8 March 2016.
[viii] "Calvin Johnson." *RamblinWreck.com*. Georgia Institute of Technology. N.d. Web.
[ix] "Freshman Faces in the Crowd." *The Technique*. Georgia Institute of Technology. 29 October 2004.
[x] Sugiura, Ken. "Reliving Calvin Johnson's Georgia Tech career." *AJC.com*. Atlanta Journal-Constitution. 1 February 2016. Web.
[xi] Wywrot, Chrissie. "Growing up in Tyrone, Ga., football wasn't Calvin Johnson's first sport." *DetroitLions.com*. Detroit Lions. 17 May 2012. Web.
[xii] Battista, Judy. "Johnson Has No Baggage and a Seat in First Class." *NYTimes.com*. New York Times. 26 April 2007. Web.
[xiii] Game notes and statistics available from *Sports-Reference.com*.
[xiv] "Georgia Tech Wins 28-24 Thriller Over No. 20 Clemson." *RamblinWreck.com*. Georgia Institute of Technology. 11 September 2004. Web.
[xv] "Calvin Johnson." *Ramblinwreck*.com. Georgia Institute of Technology. N.d. Web.
[xvi] Long, Mark. "It's all Georgia Tech in Champs Sports Bowl." *USAToday.com*. USA Today. 22 December 2004. Web.
[xvii] "Pick Four: Interceptions key to Georgia Tech win." *ESPN.com*. ESPN Internet Ventures. 4 September 2005. Web.
[xviii] Dean, Sam. "No. 4 Virginia Tech unleashes avalanche against Georgia Tech." *USAToday.com*. USA Today. 24 September 2005. Web.
[xix] "Ratliff, LaTendresse bewilder GaTech, set Utah marks." *ESPN.com*. ESPN Internet Services. 30 December 2005. Web.
[xx] Giler, Ray. "Georgia Tech's star receiver just can't miss." *USAToday.com*.

USA Today. 28 August 2006. Web.

[xxi] "Johnson snares two TDs as Georgia Tech blasts Virginia." *ESPN.com*. ESPN Internet Ventures. 22 September 2006. Web.

[xxii] "Jackets put up 38 points, upend No. 11 Hokies in Blacksburg." *ESPN.com*. ESPN Internet Ventures. 30 September 2006. Web.

[xxiii] "Ball-to-Johnson combo helps Jackets keep NC State at bay." *ESPN.com*. ESPN Internet Services. 5 November 2006. Web.

[xxiv] "Skinner, Swank lift Wake to ACC title; next stop: Orange Bowl." *ESPN.com*. ESPN Internet Services. 3 December 2006. Web.

[xxv] "Slaton not effective, but West Virginia rebounds for Gator Bowl victory." *ESPN.com*. ESPN Internet Ventures. 2 January 2007. Web.

[xxvi] "Johnson to Enter NFL Draft." *RamblinWreck.com*. Georgia Institute of Technology. 8 January 2007. Web.

[xxvii] "Midseason NFL Draft Projections." *SI.com*. Sports Illustrated. 7 February 2007. Web.

[xxviii] Game notes and statistics available from NFL.com.

[xxix] Stroud, Rick. "Georgia Tech's Johnson seen as a can't-miss WR." SPTimes.com. Tampa Bay Times. 14 February 2007.

[xxx] Clayton, John. "Johnson impresses at combine." *ESPN.com*. ESPN Internet Ventures. 26 February 2007. Web.

[xxxi] Brandt, Gil. "Individual workouts." *NFL.com*. National Football League. 16 March 2007. Web.

[xxxii] "1998 NFL Draft." *NFL.com*. National Football League. N.d. Web.

[xxxiii] "Johnson Goes to Detroit with No. 2 Pick." *RamblinWreck*.com. Georgia Institute of Technology. 28 April 2007. Web.

[xxxiv] "Top 10 Draft Surprises." *SI.com*. Sports Illustrated. 29 April 2007. Web.

[xxxv] Kowalski, Tom. "Calvin Johnson to throw first pitch at Tigers game." *Blog.MLive.com*. MLive Media Group. 29 April 2007. Web.

[xxxvi] Pasquarelli, Len. "Dungy concerned about rookies missing minicamp." *ESPN.com*. ESPN Internet Ventures. 18 May 2007. Web.

[xxxvii] Cotsonika, Nicholas. "Lions sign WR Johnson." *Freep.com*. Detroit Free Press. 3 August 2007. Web.

[xxxviii] "Quick Take: Lions hold off Raiders." *NFL.com*. National Football League. 9 September 2007. Web.

[xxxix] "Quick Take: Lions capitalize on Bucs' errors." *NFL.com*. National Football League. 21 October 2007. Web.

[xl] "Calvin Johnson shows why Lions made him No. 2 pick in the draft." *ESPN.com*. ESPN Internet Services. 22 October 2007. Web.

[xli] Kowalski, Tom. "Lions' Williams not jealous of Calvin Johnson."

MLive.com. MLive Media Group. 21 August 2008. Web.
[xlii] Kowalski, Tom. "Lions' Johnson: Back injury lingered all season."
MLive.com. MLive Media Group. 20 April 2008. Web.
[xliii] "Falcons QB Ryan, RB Turner shine in debuts vs. Lions." *ESPN.com*.
ESPN Internet Services. 8 September 2008. Web.
[xliv] "Rogers throws three TD passes as Packers beat Lions." *ESPN.com*.
ESPN Internet Services. 15 September 2008. Web.
[xlv] "Helped by pass interference penalty, Vikings win with late field goal."
ESPN.com. ESPN Internet Services. 12 October 2008. Web.
[xlvi] Yuille, Sean. "More on the Roy Williams Trade." *PrideOfDetroit.com*.
SB Nation. 15 October 2008. Web.
[xlvii] "Slaton, Daniels combine for 4 TDs as Texans hold off Lions."
ESPN.com. ESPN Internet Services. 19 October 2008. Web.
[xlviii] Samuelsen, Jamie. "Lions' Pro Bowl snub isn't all that surprising."
Freep.com. Detroit Free Press. 17 December 2008. Web.
[xlix] "2009 NFL Draft." *NFL.com*. National Football League. N.d. Web.
[l] "Matthew Stafford." *Sports-Reference.com*. Sports Reference, LLC. N.d. Web.
[li] "Detroit Lions beat Washington Redskins to end 19-game losing streak."
TheGuardian.com. The Guardian. 28 September 2009. Web.
[lii] Kowalski, Tom. "Lions beat Browns on game-winning touchdown pass by Matthew Stafford to Brandon Pettigrew." MLive.com. MLive Media Group. 22 November 2009
[liii] Seligman, Andrew. "Bears escape Lions, but not without Controversy." *NBCSports.com*. NBC Sports. 12 September 2010. Web.
[liv] "Vick's performance outshines Best's 3 TDs in Eagles' win vs. Lions." *NFL.com*. National Football League. 19 September 2010. Web.
[lv] "Lions win three straight games for first time since 2007." *ESPN.com*. ESPN Internet Ventures. 27 December 2010. Web.
[lvi] "Matthew Stafford throws for 305 yards to lead Lions past Buccaneers." *ESPN.com*. ESPN Internet Ventures. 11 September 2011. Web.
[lvii] "Lions stay unbeaten as turnovers, Calvin Johnson-fueled rally bury Cowboys." *ESPN.com*. ESPN Internet Ventures. 3 October 2011. Web.
[lviii] "Lions' O erupts as D harasses Tim Tebow in romp over Broncos." *ESPN.com*. ESPN Internet Services. 31 October 2011. Web.
[lix] "Matt Stafford leads 4th quarter rally as Lions take down Raiders." *ESPN.com*. ESPN Internet Services. 18 December 2011. Web.
[lx] "Lions bounce Chargers in romp to clinch 1st playoff berth since 1999." *ESPN.com*. ESPN Internet Services. 24 December 2011. Web.
[lxi] "Drew Brees throws for 466 yards, 3 TDs as Saints pound Lions."

ESPN.com. ESPN Internet Services. 8 January 2012. Web.
[lxii] "Calvin Johnson wins Madden vote." *ESPN.com*. ESPN Internet Services. 25 April 2012. Web.
[lxiii] "Adrian Peterson carries Minnesota Vikings past divisional rival Detroit Lions." *NFL.com*. National Football League. 28 October 2012. Web.
[lxiv] "Green Bay Packers stay in NFC North title hunt with win over Detroit Lions." *NFL.com*. National Football League. 18 November 2012. Web.
[lxv] "Andrew Luck leads Indianapolis Colts to comeback win over Detroit Lions." *NFL.com*. National Football League. 2 December 2012. Web.
[lxvi] "Calvin Johnson sets single-season receiving yards record." *NFL.com*. National Football League. 22 December 2012. Web.
[lxvii] "Chicago Bears beat Detroit Lions to stay in playoff race – for a bit." *NFL.com*. National Football League. 30 December 2012. Web.
[lxviii] "Rashard Mendenhall's late TD helps Arizona Cardinals edge Detroit Lions." *NFL.com*. National Football League. 15 September 2013. Web.
[lxix] "Detroit Lions record first ever win at Washington as Redskins fall to 0-3." *NFL.com*. National Football League. 22 September 2013. Web.
[lxx] "A.J. Green's big day carries Cincinnati Bengals past Detroit Lions." NFL.com. National Football League. 20 October 2013. Web.
[lxxi] "Stafford's sneak rallies Lions past Cowboys." NFL.com. National Football League. 27 October 2013. Web.
[lxxii] "Megatron's two TDs lead Lions past Bears." NFL.com. National Football League. 10 November 2013. Web.
[lxxiii] "Lions end Turkey Day streak with Packers' defeat." NFL.com. National Football League. 28 November 2013. Web.
[lxxiv] "Giants sneak past Lions in overtime win." NFL.com. National Football League. 22 December 2013. Web.
[lxxv] Patra, Kevin. "Detroit Lions owner William Clay Ford Sr. passes away." NFL.com. National Football League. 9 March 2014. Web.
[lxxvi] "Lions dominate Giants in Jim Caldwell's debut in Detroit." NFL.com. National Football League. 8 September 2014. Web.
[lxxvii] "Despite limited Calvin Johnson, Lions edge out Jets." NFL.com. National Football League. 28 September 2014. Web.
[lxxviii] "Lions hold off pesky Dolphins." NFL.com. National Football League. 9 November 2014. Web.
[lxxix] "Calvin Johnson shines in Detroit's 34-17 win over Chicago." NFL.com. National Football League. 27 November 2014. Web.
[lxxx] "Tony Romo, Cowboys rally past Lions in Wild Card game." NFL.com. National Football League. 4 January 2015. Web.
[lxxxi] "Controversial play allows Seattle to beat Detroit 13-10." NFL.com.

National Football League. 5 October 2015. Web.

lxxxii "Palmer, Cardinals embarrass winless Lions." NFL.com. National Football League. 11 October 2015. Web.

lxxxiii "Lions outlast Bears in overtime to nab first win." *NFL.com*. National Football League. 18 October 2015. Web.

lxxxiv Rothstein, Michael. "Calvin Johnson hits 11,000 receiving yards in record time in bad offense." *ESPN.com*. ESPN Internet Ventures. 1 November 2015. Web.

lxxxv Meinke, Kyle. "Lions WR Calvin Johnson reaches 1,000 yards receiving for sixth straight season." *MLive.com*. MLive Group. 21 December 2015. Web.

lxxxvi "Calvin Johnson's place in NFL history." *ESPN.com*. ESPN Internet Ventures. 8 March 2016. Web.

lxxxvii "Sources: Former Georgia Tech star Calvin Johnson told Lions he plans to retire." *WSBTV.com*. WSB-TV Atlanta. 31 January 2016. Web.

lxxxviii Rothstein, Michael. "Calvin Johnson retires: 'I have played my last game of football.'" *ESPN.com*. ESPN Internet Ventures. 8 March 2016.

lxxxix Rothstein, Michael. "How did Calvin Johnson reach the point of considering retirement?" *ESPN.com*. ESPN Internet Ventures. 7 January 2016.

xc Ortega, Mark. "Detroit Lions hire Bob Quinn as general manager." *NFL.com*. National Football League. 9 January 2016.

xci "Social media reaction to Calvin Johnson's retirement." *NFL.com*. National Football League. 8 March 2016.

xcii Birkett, Dave. "Lions' Corey Fuller thought Calvin Johnson was joking about retirement." *Freep.com*. Detroit Free Press. 8 April 2016.

xciii Heck, Jordan. "Barry Sanders wants to talk Calvin Johnson out of retiring." *SportingNews.com*. Sporting News. 8 April 2016.

xciv Breech, John. "Ex-Lions WR tells Calvin Johnson to unretired and sign with the Patriots." *CBSSports.com*. CBS Sports Network. 21 March 2016. Web.

xcvxcv McManamon, Pat. "Jim Caldwell says Calvin Johnson made right decision." *ESPN.com*. ESPN Internet Ventures. 23 March 2016.

xcvi Doyle, Ricky. "Will J.J. Watt Follow Calvin Johnson's Lead and Retire Early from NFL?" *NESN.com*. New England Sports Network. 6 April 2016

xcvii Kantheti, Usha. "Playing locally, serving globally." *The Technique*. Georgia Institute of Technology. 22 September 2006.

xcviii "About CJJRF." *CalvinJohnsonJrFoundation.org*. Calvin Johnson Jr. Foundation, Inc. N.d. Web.

xcix Rothstein, Michael. "How did Calvin Johnson reach the point of considering retirement?" *ESPN.com*. ESPN Internet Ventures. 7 January 2016.

[c] NFL Players Association. "Strength in Numbers." *YouTube.com*. Google. 13 November 2009.

[ci] Bonham, Chad. "Inspiring Athletes: Top Christian Sports Stories of 2012)." Beliefnet.com. Beliefnet, Inc. 28 December 2012.

[cii] DePillis, Lydia. "The Drain Catcher." *NewRepublic.com*. New Republic. 30 May 2013.

[ciii] Robinson, Brandon. "Team Give Back: Detroit Lions' Calvin Johnson, Retired NBA Baller Shaquille O'Neal and Their Moms Put their Money Where Their Mouth Is." TheSource.com. The Source. 8 July 2014.

[civ] DaSilva, Cameron. "The 10 craziest stats from Calvin Johnson's illustrious career." *FoxSports.com*. Fox Sports. 8 March 2016. Web.